Out of the Blue
A Celebration of Brockwell Park Lido
1937–2007

Peter Bradley

with Mary Hill, Dawn Henchy,

Judy Holman, Yvonne Levy,

Melanie Mauthner, Miranda Payne,

Hylda Sims, Carolyn Weniz,

Kate Aan de Wiel and Carole Woddis

Brockwell Lido Users

London 2007

Brockwell Lido Users

Published by BLUpress, PO Box 27857, London SE24 9YP, UK

www.brockwelllido.com

With funding from Lambeth Community Funds and National Lottery Awards For All

ISBN: 978-0-9556270-0-2

Front Cover: LCC Swimming Championships at Brockwell Park Lido, 1961.
Photograph Ron Chapman, by permission of London Metropolitan Archives.

Back Cover: Lido ladder, by Gethan Dick – www.gethan.org

Printed and Bound by Cambridge University Press

Designed by Martin Parker at www.silbercow.co.uk

LOTTERY FUNDED

Lambeth

Contents

~~~~~~~

Acknowledgements

Any writer is a pygmy standing on the shoulders of giants but this project stands on more shoulders (if not toes) than most. Clothing the skeleton of historical research is a wonderful body of memories, generously given by many people and carefully collected by a small group of enthusiasts.

Inevitably, the closer the present we come, the greater the number of voices. People who remember the Lido of the 1930s and 1940s are few, let alone those who swam in the lake before the opening of the Lido. Luckily, we found people who remember every decade of the Lido – and some of the lake – and each interview brought something unique that is reflected in some way here. Inevitably, we can give only a selection of what people said to us, but, being part of an oral history project, the interview tapes and transcripts are to be deposited in Lambeth Archives, where they can be savoured in full.

First thanks, then, both to those interviewed and to their interviewers, whose collaborations – which is what every good interview is – bring great riches to this book. Interviewees' names are to be found in Appendix 1. The interviewers are to be found on the title page; in addition to them, as part of a wider group preparing a Lido 70th festival for summer 2007, were Mary Fogarty and Julian Fox. Kate aan de Wiel, BLU Archivist, led the search for images both for this book and the exhibition scheduled for the Lambeth Country Show in Brockwell Park, a stone's throw from the Lido, 2007 July 21-22. Miranda Payne deserves special thanks for her work on copyright and assembling of images. Aart aan de Wiel did sterling work on archival images at the LMA. All these buoyed me up as I wrote...

For the historical research, the two archives I used most while working on this book are: Lambeth Archives Department (LAD) at the Minet Library, and the London Metropolitan Archives (LMA) off Farringdon Road. My thanks to all the staff who helped me at both institutions, but particularly to Graham Gower (who swam at the Lido in the 1950s with his school) and Len Reilly at Lambeth Archives, whose knowledge of their material is only exceeded by their kindness and professionalism. Thanks to both LAD and LMA for permission to reproduce so many images.

Anyone who writes about Lidos stands on the broad shoulders of Janet Smith, whose *Liquid Assets* was both source and inspiration.

The beautiful character of the book you hold is due to the design skills of Martin Parker of silbercow, the printing expertise of Cambridge University Press and the invaluable indexing work of Valerie Chandler.

My thanks to the staff and my fellow guests at Mount Pleasant, Reigate, where I spent a happy time creating this celebration of Brockwell Lido.

Funding for this book came from two sources, to which we are most grateful: Lambeth Community Funds and Awards for All, part of the National Lottery Funding scheme. And thanks to the Robert Holman Memorial Trust for contributions to the project. Mary Hill – unassuming non-directive leader of BLU and of the project group for this book – did the hard work to secure this funding, without which...

Peter Bradley, 2007 May 8

Rosendale School girls at the large lake in Brockwell Park for swimming lessons, 1894. The park keeper in the rowing boat is on hand to rescue swimmers in trouble. Adjoining the Walled Garden are the thatched changing sheds with canvas screens. The chimneys of the 'Temple' are smoking.

Photographer unknown. Reproduced by kind permission of London Metropolitan Archives.

Chapter 1

Swimming in the lake, 1890s–1930s

'My sister came up with me one day and she threw me into the water, into the big pond. It was the worst thing she could have done. And I went under. I never went in again. The Lido wasn't built, that was in the big pond' – Violet Irving

Before ever there was a Lido in Brockwell Park, there was, for almost 50 years, a basic swimming pool there – at the largest of the three lakes. This swimming lake was a feature of the Park from the beginning, created almost as soon as the Park was purchased, and lasting almost to the opening of the Lido in 1937.

The family that owned the Brockwell Estate sold their land off in three unequal portions between 1891 and 1903. The purchase of the biggest portion, two-thirds, of the Estate went through on Maundy Thursday, 1891 and the new park was thrown open to the public the next day, Good Friday, March 28.

The official opening by Lord Rosebery, Chairman of the London County Council (LCC), was not for 15 months (Whit Monday Bank Holiday, 1892 June 6). But in autumn of the first year of the Park's existence, the LCC was presented with a petition, by local LCC Councillor Evan Spicer (later to donate the – now vanished – drinking fountain near the Clock Tower), "from ratepayers and inhabitants of Herne Hill and the vicinity, asking the Council to form a lake in Brockwell Park".[11] At this stage, the glorious lakes of previous days had dwindled into a miserable mere with rickety fencing.[12]

The LCC batted this petition to the relevant committee, Parks & Open Spaces, which duly discussed it on 1891 November 13 (the same meeting discussed a – fortunately short-lived – proposal "to turn the Walled Garden into a tennis court").

The LCC had only been set up itself in 1891 and from the outset had this Parks Committee. So here was both a London-wide body with the power and finances to make things happen – and a committee devoted to parks and anxious to prove its worth. Noting that the residents near Brockwell Park had been in favour of a lake being formed in the park "large enough to enable such pastimes as model yachting", the full Council voted £490 (around £33,000 today) for the formation of a lake, carrying also an amendment "that the Committee be requested to consider whether suitable arrangements can be made for bathing".[13] It's interesting to see how closely involved the LCC was with the minutiae of arrangements in a local park. Its successor, the GLC, disdained such involvement, speedily devolving London's parks to local authorities in 1971. The variations in the balance of power between a London-wide authority – and occasionally national government – and the local council were to be played out over the next century, down to our own day.

Rosendale School boys at the large lake in Brockwell Park for swimming lessons, 1894.
Some are wearing full swimming costumes, some just slips. On the perimeter, to left of
centre, a substantial fountain that has long gone; houses of Tulse Hill in the distance.

Photographer unknown. Reproduced by kind permission of London Metropolitan Archives.

The Parks Committee duly considered the Council's request and on 1892 February 5 came to the conclusion "that this can be done without any extra expense" – penny-pinching being another common theme down the ages – and "have accordingly directed the Architect to make the lower lake of a suitable depth for bathing, and to form gravel banks".[14] I haven't been able to discover when the lake was constructed but it sounds as if plans were in hand, so it could have been ready by summer of 1892, in time for the official opening.

Certainly, by 1894, the swimming lake in Brockwell Park was a fixture, coming before the LCC for debate twice. At its April 27 meeting, the Parks Committee had in front of it a request from the School Board of London. "Anxious to encourage the art of swimming amongst the elementary [ie primary] schools", the Board asked the LCC to allow children exclusive use of its "various bathing places". It recommended that, as an experiment, children would be allowed to bathe until 9am on Saturdays in the lakes at Brockwell Park, Clapham Common

HEALTH My 94-year-old Dad used to swim in the lido as a dapper young man and there are still people made of his resilience who take a bracing swim at 7am and who may indeed live just as long as he has. – **Becka Thackray (L55)**

PEACE My lifeline at times **(S679)**

NB: In this book, the prefix 'L' – refers to the 70+ Lido interviews with named individuals, conducted in 2006–2007. The prefix 'S' refers to the 800+ people who took part in the BLU Survey in 2001, who were guaranteed anonymity, and so are referred to by their survey number.

and Hampstead Heath, and the LCC agreed.[15]

One local school at least took up the opportunity: there are wonderful photos of children from Rosendale Road School swimming in the lake at Brockwell Park in 1897.[16] As was always the case at the lake, right up to 1935, these were single-sex excursions. In one photo, about three dozen Rosendale girls in swimming costume are sedately posed on the diving board and jetty. There is a park keeper in a rowing boat – ready to the rescue, if needed – and five girls actually in the water. There are screens on the thatched changing rooms (which were built against the wall of the Walled Garden) and a chimney on the 'Temple' is smoking. Of their sex, only girls were allowed to bathe in the lake at this period; adult women weren't allowed in until 1929. In the boys' photo, about 18 youths are disporting themselves in the water slightly less sedately. Their clothes appear to have been left on benches.

The second 1894 appearance of Brockwell Park swimming lake was on July 24, when Councillor Hubbard presented a petition to the full Council "to allow bathing in the lake in Brockwell Park in the evening as well as the morning". Again, the petition "from young men resident in the neighbourhood of Brockwell Park" was referred to Parks & Open Spaces, which discussed it on October 12. Not for the last time, the Committee decided that the conflicting interests of other park lovers – the evening was a time "when the park is largely used by general visitors" – meant it could not "grant the prayer of the memorial", a refusal the full Council endorsed.[17]

Another constant theme – water quality – makes its first appearance in 1896, with a petition to the Council asking it "to remedy the insanitary condition of the bathing-lake at Brockwell Park; to extend the lake so as to include the upper duck-ponds; to increase the dressing accommodation, and also to provide another diving board".[18] Like the 1894 young men's petition for evening opening, this 1896 one indicates a constituency of swimmers engaged enough to ask for more… The robust LCC politicians on the Parks Committee said "we were already aware that the lake needed attention" and had sanctioned the cleaning out of the lake, but "did not think it necessary at present to increase the accommodation".[19]

The next year, 1897, bathing hours at the LCC's lakes "which… will not materially interfere with the use of the places by the general public" were set as: before 8am on weekdays and before 9am on Sundays. Although these hours might seem ungenerous to us, there are reports of there being summer access from 4am, which makes it a more reasonable proposition. The sessions were, as mentioned, single-sex only and, as Janet Smith says, at this period that meant largely men only and – frequently – men who were naked.[1.10] As late as 1920, there's a broad hint that nudity was the rule rather than the exception, at least for boys, in Brockwell Park. A humorous piece in the *Brixton Free Press* imagines a pheasant telling a magpie (two of the birds in the Park aviary (which was next to the changing shed, says David Hamley (L28))[1.11] that "he might have his peace of mind disturbed in the summer when the large crowds of children come to bathe, and, if he is a very sensitive bird, his notion of propriety might be somewhat disturbed when little 'Erb disrobes 'to take the cure' "!"[1.12] There are suggestions that it was possible to close access to the lake when swimming was allowed, presumably on the grounds of modesty. Such

ARCHITECTURE The buildings? "I love them. I think they are great. They are quintessentially lido buildings… they are perfect… they move perfectly with the water…" – **Theresa Hoare (L31)**

I remember floating in the water and looking up at these tower blocks which are actually very close to the pool and they are a reminder of how fantastic it is that the pool is there especially for the people living in the tower blocks, to be able to make use of the facility. – **Janet Smith (L52)**

I like the fact that it's big. That even when it's hot you can swim about. There's a great lifting of my spirits when I know it's going to open. It gives me a change of perspective. – **Ruth Thompson (L56)**

closure would also explain why the LCC was anxious to minimise the occasions when the general public would be denied access to the full park.

David Hamley swam in the lake himself: "But this big pond was used for a swimming pool. The men used to go up there and change underneath the shelter. By the aviary there was a long shelter and people used to go and change in there and swim in this pond. There was a little diving board. You could go anytime. Much depended on the weather. As children we weren't allowed to go in there unless our Dad was with us. It was mainly the boys and the men who would partake of this swimming because the water was rather dirty and muddy you know, it was not hygienic so the new swimming pool came…"

There are occasional references to "summer" and "winter" seasons at the LCC lakes. There may have been brief closures for maintenance but they seem to have been swum in all year round. Writing about Brockwell Park in 1920, WJ Perrin mentions "the all-the-year-round bather – and I have been numbered amongst them for the past twenty years" [ie back to 1900].[1.13]

Proof royal of the popularity of the facility came on two occasions in 1898, first when the Parks Committee meeting on July 22 agreed to the concreting of the lake "in view of the extent to which the lake in Brockwell-park is used for the purpose of bathing, and the inconvenience which the bathers suffer owing to the stirring up of the mud". The full Council voted £1000 (£80,000 today) for this work.[1.14] The concreting work took two years to complete.[1.15] Two classic British excuses were given for the delay. "the peculiar nature of the bottom of the lake, which could not be ascertained

until the lake was emptied" and "excessive heat during July", followed by "the storms of July and August".[1.16]

The second, delightful, proof was the Committee's decision at the same 1898 meeting to propose an amendment of the Park Byelaws, that prohibited cycling within the Park. The full Council adopted this resolution: "That persons going to bathe in the lake at Brockwell-park be permitted to ride their cycles over the paths leading to the lake up to 8 o'clock a.m." It conjures up a vision of Victorian commuters impatiently grabbing their swim before cycling to work – and damn the byelaws! As late as 1933, the byelaw was changed again, to allow cycling up to 9.15am.[1.17]

In 1900, the Brockwell Park thatched bathing shelter was "in an extremely dilapidated condtion" and the LCC agreed £100 (£8000 today) for repairs.[1.18]

A bold bid for total swimmer power was made at a full Council meeting on 1902 January 28, with a motion asking the Parks & Open Spaces Committee "to permit of the use of any pieces of water within their jurisdiction for bathing during the whole time that these pieces of water are open to the public".[1.19]

The Committee's leisurely response (June 20) was minimalist, agreeing to extend bathing hours at Brockwell Park on Monday and Thursday to 11am. The extension was said to be in response to a letter from "Mr Lyell, honorary secretary of the Gresham Swimming Club".[1.20] This is the first record I have found of a specific club in connection with the lake. More than one club seems to have used it: in 1908, the 'Brockwell Park Swimming Club' announced in the *Brixton Free Press* that it had "opened a juvenile branch for boys under the age of 16".[1.21] It also

Postcard of Brockwell Park swimming lake, 1900–1909. The immense popularity of the lake is shown in this image. Park byelaws were changed to allow swimmers to cycle to the lake, hence the number of bikes. Although children of both sexes could swim there (though not together), only adult males were admitted at this period. Women were allowed to swim in the lake from 1929.

Photographer unknown. © English Heritage, Nigel Temple Postcard Collection.

illustrates how history is not all progress; there has been no swimming club at the Lido at all since the 1994 re-opening.

Evidence of the limited opportunities for women in the LCC's open air lakes comes in 1902, when the Council agreed, "as an experiment", to allow women sole use of the lake at Parliament Hill on Wednesdays, "subject to their wearing the costume approved by the ASA [Amateur Swimming Association]".[1.22] The progress of women in open air swimming in the old lakes was slow – in 1903, asked to allow bathing "by both sexes all day at all bathing places, subject to proper costumes being worn", the LCC concluded "it would not be desirable at present to extend the existing facilities for bathing by men and women".[1.23] There was never equal access – a state of affairs even perpetuated in the opening hour regulations for the 1937 Lido (see Chapter 3). And the municipal obsession with regulating what swimmers could wear – and the ASA's role in policing it – was to be a frequent theme right up to the Second World War.

Here are two typical LCC reports from the costume wars, the first this deadpan minute from 1935: "No action to be taken on the suggestion of the Men's Dress Reform Party that the bathing regulations should be amended so as to allow male bathers to wear slips only at all times."[1.24] And in

BEACH London is not close to a beach so the pool is the only escape for me (**S35**). It is the closest thing to a city beach (**S256**). It is a beach in the city (**S330**).

Like being on a holiday which was affordable which was not very far and you could go with your friends so my memory is like, just like fun – **Cindy Afflict (L1)**

'The Lido is different and it's nice, we're getting nice summers – the whole décor of it almost made me feel I was home… it had that Caribbean feel – it's the sort of thing we do in the West Indies – it's like a beach. A place to bathe and where you can sit out and have a drink – the next best thing to not having the sun and the sea. – **Hilda Castillo-Binger (L12)**

Photograph by James Perrin, 2006 July 19, courtesy of *South London Press*

1936: "We have allowed men to bathe in short costumes during mixed bathing." This wouldn't have applied to Brockwell Park lake, where there was no mixed bathing, although by 1936 it had been closed to bathing anyway.[125]

Whatever about adults and their threateningly saucy ways, it seems to have been more acceptable that girls as well as boys should learn to swim, though not, of course, together. In November 1904, the LCC allotted school children two hours, 9am-11am (ie one hour apiece), at Brockwell Park on one day a week.[126] Next year, another LCC committee, Education, went into precise detail about the

implementation of this policy, noting that some local head teachers had been "somewhat reluctant to arrange for swimming instruction… in the open air under the existing conditions". A rope had to be stretched across the shallow end, a portion of the changing rooms had to be screened off for teachers and there had to be a boatman on hand "in order to ensure their safety". The day chosen was Tuesday, with boys first at 9am, a transition from the early morning men-only session, and girls at 10am. The public was to be excluded and teachers were to select "only robust children".[127]

It was a huge success. In the summer of 1905,

RELAXATION Cressingham Gardens Estate Senior Citizens group came up with their memories. **Melody Carter (L11)**'s best memory (1950s): "When someone tried to push me in the deep end and I screamed!" **Lily Legrice (L38)**, born 1917, remembers the fountain and that the area was full of "well-behaved, respectable people". **Rose Mitchell (L44)**, born 1930: "You used to be able to hire towels for about 2 old pence [less than 1p]". Because they lived on Dulwich Road they could see the Lido queue, then up the steps on the main road, from their front windows. They would wait until the queue was of a manageable length and then quickly walk across the road to the Lido.

5584 boys and 1142 girls bathed in the lake during the school holidays: "We therefore propose to make similar arrangements in future years."[1.28]

Violet Irving (L17), born 1917, remembers the lake well: "There used to be the big end where the board was, that was for the divers. The other end was for the youngsters, like such as me. I never learned to swim… they used to have canopies, where you used to undress. On the other side was the paddling pond. I was just a schoolkid. If you had an accident they took you to the big house. My sister came up with me one day and she threw me into the water, into the big pond. It was the worst thing she could have done. And I went under. I never went in again. The Lido wasn't built, that was in the big pond."

Jack King (L37) remembers swimming in the large pond in Brockwell Park as a child right up to 1937, two years after the LCC supposedly closed it to swimmers. He and his sister used to go over early on Sunday mornings in the summer, usually between 7 and 9: "The pond had an 8ft diving board and the area below it had been dug out to a depth of 6 or 8ft to make it safe for diving. On Sundays two big temporary screens were put up for changing – one for men and the other for women. There was a man on duty to make certain that everyone behaved and to pull out anyone who got into difficulties by rowing out to them in the boat that was kept on the pond."

When the Lido was built in 1937 and swimming was no longer allowed in the pond, men used to bring their model speed boats and yachts with steam or combustion engines and spent many hours sailing and racing the boats around the pond, King said.

The lake at Brockwell Park continued in popular use right up to the 1930s. It appears regularly in Council minutes, when repairs are needed or regulations require adjusting. In 1907, the LCC reduced Sunday opening hours from 9am to 8am "in view of the desirability of allowing the public to use the paths near the pond… at an earlier hour"* [*LCC Minutes of Proceedings, 1907 December 17, p1402.], only to have to revise it up to 8.30am the following year, presumably after "representations" by hardy but bolshy winter bathers.[1.29] In 1910, robbing Peter to pay Paul, the LCC Finance Committee appropriated £25 (£1800 today) intended for renewing lamps on the Park's bandstand "to meet the cost of the high diving-board at the bathing lake".[1.30] And in 1911, the cost of extra water to the lake during a summer drought, "owing to the abnormal use of the lake during hot weather" was £52.10s.6d (£52.52½p – £3700 today).[1.31] New 'granolithic' paving was installed to the surround of the lake in 1926,[1.32] while in 1928 yet another request – this time from the Metropolitan Borough of Lambeth (it didn't own the Park, the LCC did) – for mixed bathing at the lake in Brockwell Park was rejected.[1.33] In 1928 too, with brilliant timing, the LCC emptied the lake in June. 'The Bathers' Lament' was the title for a photograph of it in a local paper. The caption said it all: "Holiday visitors to Brockwell Park in the empty basin of the swimming pool. Local bathers were keenly disappointed in not being able to enjoy their morning dip during the recent spell of brilliant sunshine. Could not this necessary work be carried out earlier in the year and not during the holiday season?"[1.34] A *cri de coeur* that echoes down the years.

The late 1920s/early 1930s saw tinkering with the opening hours – longer and later, including

Photo: Miranda Payne

should be discontinued forthwith".[138] With huge numbers swimming in what is actually quite a small lake, water quality in the capital got to the point that in June 1934 the LCC ordered the closure to bathers (though not to toy yachts) of its lakes at Brockwell Park, Plumstead Common and Victoria Park.[139] The ban barely lasted the summer. The Parks Committee mournfully reported: "As a result of requests from local residents, bathing for men has been allowed daily up to 9am in the lake at Brockwell Park from October, 1934… subject to the condition of the water."[140] At its meeting on 1935 April 16, the Committee noted that "the condition of the water speedily deteriorated" and bathing was again prohibited. The Parks Committee declined to act on Councillor WF Marchant's suggestion that the lake again be cleaned out.[141]

This was the death blow for swimming in the lake at Brockwell Park. Jeffrey Rumble, in his *A Brockwell Boy*, describes how both fish and humans were found to have eye infections from the lake.[142] With the 1936 *Public Health Act*, new water standards would render the old Victorian bathing lakes illegal.

Fortunately, help was at hand. The Parks Committee may have been signing the lake's death warrant in April 1935. In the same month it had also ordered the placing of adverts in *The Builder*, *Contract Journal* and *Daily Telegraph*, inviting tenders for one of the LCC's most ambitious sports projects – the construction of a new open-air swimming pool at Brockwell Park – later to be called the Lido.[143] By May the following year, contractors were breaking the ground by the Dulwich Road…

evenings. And the roaring Twenties finally reached the lake in 1929, when the male bastion crumbled and, for the first time, women were allowed to bathe there, in single-sex sessions on Tuesday, Thursday and Saturday mornings. Special canvas screens were put up in the changing sheds to protect them from prying eyes. Girls of school age had of course been allowed to swim there since the 1890s.[135]

A sign of the times, the unemployed were used to do work in the Park in general and at the lake in particular in this decade.[136]

As so often with open air swimming in Britain, the death blow for the lake at Brockwell Park came from the weather. Not, for once, bad weather, but from the heatwave summers of 1933 and 1934, which adversely affected water quality. First, the Parks Committee proposed to close the lake after the end of the winter season 1933-34.[137] That doesn't seem to have gone down well with the locals because by April, the Committee had decided to empty, clean and refill the lake "with fresh water to which the chlorination process… was to be applied". If water quality deteriorated, "bathing

Timeline 1: Swimming in the lake, 1890s–1930s

1891 MARCH 28 Two-thirds of Brockwell Estate purchased as public park, which opens on Good Friday **OCTOBER** Locals petition LCC to create pond in Brockwell Park for toy yachting **1892 FEBRUARY** LCC Parks Committee votes to make pond also suitable for bathing **JUNE** Park officially opened by Lord Rosebery, chair of LCC. Thomas Lynn Bristowe MP, who led the campaign to create the Park, dies after the opening **1894 APRIL** Schoolchildren allowed exclusive use of LCC lakes on Saturday mornings **JULY** Local young men's petition for evening swims rejected by LCC **1896 OCTOBER** Petition about insanitary conditions; lake cleaned out **1898 JULY** LCC agreed to concreting of lake (work not completed till 1900) and amended byelaws to allow cyclists to ride to lake before 8am **1904 NOVEMBER** School-children allotted two hours' single-sex bathing per week **1908 JUNE** 'Brockwell Park Swimming Club' opens juvenile branch for boys **1910 JULY** £25 voted for high diving-board at lake **1920 NOVEMBER** Unemployment grant 'for cleaning out of lake' **1926 APRIL** New 'granolithic' paving installed around the lake **1928 JUNE** Pool emptied in high summer **DECEMBER** LCC rejects MBL request for mixed bathing at the lake **1929 APRIL** Women (as opposed to girls who swam in the lake from 1894) allowed to bathe in the lake for the first time **1930 DECEMBER** Unemployment grant 'for mudding out ponds' **1933** LCC writes to MBL, warning of insanitary conditions at lake; offered to allocate site for modern open-air bath near Rosendale Road **1934 FEBRUARY** LCC proposed closure of lake due to poor water **APRIL** Lake to be emptied and refilled with chlorinated water **JUNE** Lake closed to bathers **OCTOBER** Lake re-opened 'as a result of requests from local residents' **1935 APRIL** Bathing at lake again prohibited and for the final time; LCC invites tenders for new open-air swimming bath at Brockwell Park...

Mary Datchelor Girls School swimming team with Lambeth's Mayor EA Mills JP on the Lido's opening day, 1937 July 10, when they put on a diving and synchronised swimming display. The caption said: 'The Mayor with a bevy of bathing belles at the opening of the swimming pool.' Thelma Phelps – thrown into the pool by the Mayor to inaugurate the pool – has her arms round the Mayor's neck. *Brixton Free Press*, 1937 July 16.

Chapter 2

Towards the Lido: The 1920s/1930s campaign for open-air bathing in Lambeth

"…being unanimously of opinion that open air bathing is an invigorating and healthful form of recreation which should be encouraged…" – Metropolitan Borough of Lambeth's Public Health Committee, 1929

The 1920s was a period of mixed fortunes in the UK and elsewhere – high unemployment on the one hand and a new search for leisure for ordinary people on the other. In London's municipal politics, the relationship between the central body, the London County Council (LCC), and the metropolitan boroughs, such as Lambeth (MBL) – never an easy one – was put under strain, the local boroughs testing the limits of their powers, the powerful LCC not rushing to yield. So although Brockwell Park was in the Borough of Lambeth, which had definite views about the Park as a local resource, it was owned and administered in a very hands-on fashion by the central authority. Out of the dynamics of that central vs local relationship, the 1937 Lido was born.

The first faint impetus to action came in the form of Motion 51, passed by the LCC on 1923 March 20. It asked: "That, in connection with the question of unemployment in London, it be referred to the Special Committee on Unemployment and the Parks & Open Spaces Committee to consider and report whether or not the construction of an open-air bath in Brockwell-park should be put in hand directly by the Council or in conjunction with other

authorities."[2.1] The movers, Councillors Gosling (appropriately enough), and RCE Powell, were making a point about unemployment, but were also quite innovative in their idea for tackling it. At that stage, there was no 'lido mania' in the country, although the biggest swimming pool in the world, at Blackpool, was nearing completion (it opened in June) and they may have had in mind the success of the 1906 Tooting Bec pool. In 1931, Kennington's Lido would be built largely by unemployed labour, but this was a radical thought in 1923.

The Parks & Open Spaces Committee slapped down the idea, "in view of the good facilities for bathing already provided at this park".[2.2] Had their proposal gone ahead, Brockwell Park would probably have had a more simple, basic facility.

The next move, five years on, was by the Metropolitan Borough of Lambeth (MBL)'s wonderfully named Baths & Cemetery Committee (B&CC). A Council meeting on 1928 October 18 had agreed with B&CC's recommendation to write to the LCC urging it, "in view of the vastly increased popularity in swimming, to enlarge and extend the facilities for bathing, especially mixed bathing, at the

COMMUNITY Paddy was brilliant, I like to think I taught him some childcare skills. –
Helen Fensterheim (L24)

It's like a small dream come true… it's such a community thing, in the best park in the whole of this borough, it's been given a new lease of life… to me, it's like the heart pumping inside the body… everything will be drawn to it. – **Theresa Hoare (L31)**

Photo: Miranda Payne

lake in Brockwell Park".[23] There was, of course, no mixed bathing at the lake at the time, so it was a trend-setting request by Lambeth. The Clerk of the LCC replied on December 7 in measured terms, saying that mixed bathing would provoke "an immediate demand for the provision of cubicles, as experience has proved that the majority of women bathers will not use an open shelter". Surrounding the lake with cubicles would destroy the lake's "ornamental character", while all-day bathing would make it necessary "to exclude the general public from the lake enclosure". The lake at Brockwell Park, he added, was not comparable to the pool at Tooting Common, which, he pointed out, "was specially constructed as a swimming bath, to which bathers only have access, and its presence does not interfere with public enjoyment or recreation".[24]

Nothing daunted, B&CC put down a marker at its 1929 January 24 meeting: "…the question was raised as to the public health aspect of such facilities". It was an important phrase, as for the next decade, the public health benefits of open-air swimming were to become a national (and indeed European) obsession. This hint was naturally picked up by Lambeth's Public Health Committee, which conceded that the LCC "no" to an improved lake might have been actuated "by reasons which doubtless appeared to it quite valid". It recommended MBL to approach the LCC about creating facilities for open-air bathing at Kennington, Norwood and Brockwell Parks ("or… at any other Park… within the Borough"), "being unanimously of opinion that open air bathing is an invigorating and healthful form of recreation which should be encouraged" – and on 1929 March 7 the full Lambeth Council endorsed its recommendation.[2.5] In its reply of 1929 May 10, the LCC remained unenthusiastic, pointing out that it had recently increased opening hours at the Brockwell Park lake, including "summer bathing by women, which has not hitherto been allowed". The sting was in the tail: "…the principle upon which that Authority [ie the LCC] has proceeded for some years past as regards the construction of such baths, has been that the Local Authority concerned [ie Lambeth] should bear the cost of construction and half the cost of the maintenance of the bath."[2.6] In other words, MBL would have to put its money where its mouth was.

The Brockwell Park scheme was put on hold while Lambeth devoted its energies to negotiating with the LCC for the construction of a pool in the new extension to Kennington Park. This involved unemployed labour. It was completed in 1931 and proved a great success. Lambeth continued to explore the possibility of open-air pools in Norwood and Brockwell Parks, but if it was Lambeth proposing, it was definitely LCC disposing. A 1931 LCC Valentine's Day letter to MBL finally concluded "that Norwood Park is unsuitable for such a purpose". The LCC sweetened the blow: "If… the Lambeth Borough Council thinks it well to suggest a site at another Park", the LCC would consider it.[2.7]

However, it was the LCC that precipitated matters, so to speak. On 1933 December 11, it wrote to MBL: "Examinations last summer [ie 1933] of the water in the concreted lake at Brockwell Park have disclosed a serious state of affairs as regards its sanitary condition. As you are aware… the lake is very much frequented by bathers." It concluded that any adaptation to make the lake suitable for bathing "under modern conditions" would be "expensive and unsatisfactory".[2.8] If it was preparing to close one door (a decision fought by local swimmers), it was ready to open another. The LCC, as the strategic authority – and owner of Brockwell Park – was prepared, it said, under the usual conditions, "to allocate a suitable site in the park for the construction of an open-air swimming bath, with filtration plant and all the appurtenances of an up-to-date bath for use as an alternative to the existing bathing lake". The usual conditions were that MBL would bear the full costs of construction, estimated at £12,500 and half the £800 cost of annual maintenance. The LCC proposed to impose charges for using the pool – the lake had always been free – tempting MBL with the suggestion that as a result "it is within the bounds of possibility that there may be no maintenance costs at all". The Chief Officer of the LCC Parks Department "has come to the conclusion that free bathing is unsatisfactory, as on free bathing days a considerable amount of damage is done to the cubicles, etc".[2.9]

The design would be similar to Kennington's, but £2300 more expensive than it because of improvements such as an extended surround "to prevent fouling of the water by persons walking adjacent thereto with their ordinary shoes or boots on" and "a locker scheme in connection with a Changing Hut".[2.10]

The proposed site for the new bath was adjacent

Handtinted card of the Lido, c. 1938. The great Chas Wicksteed & Co diving platform is at the deep end, with a smaller board on the café side. This is one of two flowerbeds in front of the café, adorned by bathing belle in a daring outfit. By this stage, the rigid regulations about full costumes are breaking down.

Photograph by W Chamberlain, from www.lambethlandmark.com. Reproduced by kind permission of Lambeth Archives.

to the Norwood Road, north-east of the Rosendale Road entrance of Brockwell Park.

The Baths & Cemetery Committee concluded that "the Borough Council would be well advised to accept the offer". In under four years – not bad going for a municipal project – the pool would be a reality.

Lambeth formally voted to accept the offer on 1934 January 29, with the important rider "that further enquiries be made of the [LCC] Parks Department as to the advisability of extending the scope and amenities of the Scheme".[2.11] This was a crucial decision that shaped the final design; it meant that Lambeth was not content simply to repeat what had been done at Kennington – it was thinking big.

The LCC wrote back on February 26, pointing out that the provision of terraces for spectators would increase the size and cost of the pool but Lambeth insisted on "amenities which are now commonly provided, viz., accommodation for spectators, sun bathing area, refreshment rooms, etc" – all of which were eventually incorporated in the final design.

A consequence of a larger design was that the LCC no longer considered the Rosendale Road site appropriate. On July 3, the LCC's Chief Officer of the Parks Department (COPD) wrote to MBL that "a better and more commodious position for the bath would be on the field on the Dulwich Road boundary".[2.12] Osmond Cattlin, Lambeth's Borough Engineer, the lead officer for the pool project, agreed, saying the site was "the most suitable, and one which would not interfere to any great extent with the existing natural beauties and characteristics of the Park".

On 1934 July 27, there was a summer outing for the LCC Parks Committee, which "met at County Hall and proceeded by motor car to visit… Brockwell Park". While there, the Committee examined both the original site at Rosendale Road and the final choice at Dulwich Road.[2.13]

Following a meeting between Lambeth's Engineer, Cattlin, and the LCC's lead architect for the planned pool, HA Rowbotham, the COPD wrote confirming that Lambeth's suggested additional facilities had been incorporated in the plan, comprising "sun bathing area, refreshment room, terrace for spectators including separate lavatory accommodation." Thought had been given to spectacle: the spectators' entrances had an attendant's box beside them to take money for Gala events and a "committee room would be available when Gala displays are given", while "some form of barrier or fencing could be fixed

between the bath area and the public space to separate bathers and spectators". All bathers would enter through chlorinated wading pools. A modern filtration plant offering a 4/5 hour turnover "would be desirable". It is clear that even before a final decision on financing or location had been taken, the LCC's plans for a modern pool were well in hand.

But of course the LCC wouldn't be paying, so on 1934 August 23 the COPD reminded Lambeth that these new features meant that the original figure of £12,500 "cannot stand". He estimated the new cost at almost double, £23,000 (about £1 million today) and said he would be "glad to hear as soon as possible if your Council approve the plans generally in order that the work can go forward".[2.14]

The Lambeth Councillors initially didn't jib so much at the new cost, as at the change of location from Rosendale Road. COPD wrote back patiently on 1934 October 16 to say that Rosendale Road had been the preferred site when the size of the pool was smaller. Building the new pool with "amenities" there would entail removal of "a line of well-established trees on the north side", cutting into higher ground and "falling leaf nuisance" on the south side. You get an image of a public official who has made their mind up…[2.15] Unabashed, MBL Councillors Mallinson and Bagnall voted to ask him to look even further in the Park, to a site at Brockwell Park Gardens. While waiting for a site decision, councillors discussed the plan, reducing the sun-bathing area and deleting the rest room. Ambulance room, committee room, spectator terrace and café and tea terrace were all approved – and all are to be found in the final design.

The dithering about the site of the pool stopped at the end of 1934. COPD pointed out to Lambeth that at the Brockwell Park Gardens site "the levels of the ground… are so steep that it would increase the cost of the Bath and seriously injure the facilities for both football and cricket". In a letter dated 1934 November 26, COPD bluntly asked "if your Council accepts the site on the Dulwich Road boundary", cleverly but perhaps not very ethically promising that if this point were settled he would "go closely into the matter of cost and see what can be done to reduce the figure to a maximum of £20,000". At its meeting on 1935 January 7, the Baths & Cemetery Committee crumbled. It agreed to recommend to the full Lambeth Council that it accept the Dulwich Road site and the expenditure of £23,000 "for an open-air swimming bath in Brockwell Park". The full Lambeth Council adopted its recommendation on 1935 January 31.[2.16] On February 15, a major meeting of the LCC's Parks Committee sealed the deal with Lambeth, forwarding MBL "a detailed plan", asking the LCC Solicitor to draft an agreement with MBL and ordering the preparation of tenders.[2.17]

The LCC was going full steam ahead with the project. A call for tenders was sent out in April, for return by August.[2.18] An interesting condition was that bidders were required to give alternative sets of estimates: (i) if materials came from any source; (ii) if they were "wholly from, and manufactured entirely within, the British Empire".[2.19]

In the middle of all this, on 1935 April 16, the Brockwell Park lake was shut to bathers, never to re-open as a swimming pool – with keen swimmers having to wait over two years for the Lido to open.[2.20] At the end of the year, the lake was even to suffer the humiliation of being designated as a 'shoot' ie dumping area for spoil excavated from the new Lido.[2.21] It's not certain that actually happened;

after all a viable lake is still there today. And David Hamley (L28) – who as a builder by trade should know – recalls differently: "They would be digging this out and they wheeled the spoil, the stuff they had excavated, over to a place just about where you go into the car park from the park today. There used to a little park keeper's lodge there at the bottom of the gate and it was near there that they had this heap of stuff and it was all taken away by horse and cart. I don't remember it being taken away by lorry." Perhaps some was used to reduce the deep end of the lake.

On 1935 September 9, the Chairman of the LCC Parks Committee opened the 17 sealed tenders received. In all bids, there was no variation in price between global (i) and patriotic, imperial (ii) estimates.

Having swallowed the cost of £23,000, MBL spent 1935 haggling over the annual maintenance costs and how any profits would be shared between it and the LCC. MBL also tried to get the LCC to agree the new pool would not be closed for more than a week without MBL's consent. It got short shrift, the LCC crisply saying it would decide when and why the pool needed closing: "…the arrangements made by the [LCC]… over a period of years… are in the best interests of the public and the [LCC] does not… feel that the suggestion of the Borough Council is one that it can adopt."[2.22]

Perhaps as a result of such haggling from Lambeth and other boroughs, the LCC decided in 1935 October that from 1936 April 1 it would bear all maintenance costs of all open-air baths (garnering all profits too, of course). It would also in future halve all construction costs between itself and any borough proposing to build an open-air bath "as they have a particular value for the

HAVEN/OASIS To me the Lido represents freedom in the city and that extraordinary experience at 9 o'clock in the morning with a practically empty pool, a beautiful sunny day, just swimming up and down, feeling at one with one's surroundings, feeling incredibly privileged that there is this oasis in the city which is so welcoming, where you can hang out and have a cup of tea and chat to old friends, but also make new ones. And then there's that sense of community. I think these public spaces should be a public space, a public democratic space. They are places to be cherished at a time of increasing privatisation of everything in the city. – **Rose de Wend Fenton (L20)**

Photo: Miranda Payne

inhabitants of the locality".[2.23]

In the embers of 1935, Lambeth saw its chance. As construction of the Brockwell Park bath had not yet started, why couldn't the LCC apply its cost-sharing scheme for constructing open-air pools retrospectively? If it did, Lambeth might consider yielding and permitting the LCC to take all the costs – and profits – of annual maintenance from it. Part of MBL's *angst* around the deal was that costs for the pool – all of which it had to bear – had risen from the original £23,000 to £27,000, which it was obliged by the agreement to pay in full – and which it presumably felt could rise even higher by the time of completion – but you have to admire their

chutzpah even as you tremble at their temerity.[2.24]

The LCC's reply was not swift but it was inexorable. On 1936 January 31 it wrote to say that the agreement between MBL and LCC had been concluded "so long ago as February... and... subsequent arrangements had been advanced and completed upon such basis". In all the circumstances, "the County Council regretted that it could not see its way to modify the existing agreement for the bath at Brockwell Park, and would be glad to learn that the Borough Council was willing to concur in the proposal to accept a tender for the work...."[2.25]

A couple of weeks later, on 1936 March 14, the

Lido

The use of the word 'lido' to describe an open-air swimming pool seems to be an exclusively British thing and largely a creation of the 1930s. Or, as the *Cambridge Advanced Learner's Dictionary* puts it: "Mainly UK Old-fashioned."

The first pool to be called a Lido in the UK was the Serpentine Lido in 1930, the brainchild of Labour MP George Lansbury, who "actively promoted the rights of working people to outdoor recreation"[2.38] (though there had been swimming facilities at the Serpentine since 1730). As described in Chapter 3, 'Lido mania' hit Britain in the 1930s: the transformation of London, in particular, into a 'City of Lidos' was a main policy plank of the ruling Labour group on the LCC.

To call an open air pool in a cold clime a 'Lido' was to borrow in hope the glamour and sexiness of the Lido of Venice. This is an island reef separating the Venice lagoon from the open Adriatic, protecting Venice from flooding and historically acting as a defensive barrier against attack. By the Belle Epoque of the late 19th/early 20th century, its beaches and its hotels had turned the sand spit of the Lido into a fashionable resort. Its Hotel des Bains was the setting for Thomas Mann's 1912 *Death in Venice* – and the word 'Lido' achieved European fame.

The Italian word 'lido' ('lito' in medieval times or poetically) historically meant "the last spit of land, where the waves beat". Dante used it in his *Paradiso*: "Tornate a riveder li vostri liti" ("Return to see your shores again")[2.39] But in modern Italy it refers to a beach with bar, beach chairs etc – parallel to the English usage of a lido being a pool with "extras", such as café, sunbathing terrace. So the Lido of Venice is only the most magnificent example of a phenomenon common to the whole Italian seaboard.

The Italian word in turn comes from the Latin 'litus' – a shore (same root as 'littoral').

The first edition of the *Oxford English Dictionary* (L Volume, 1901–03) was not yet alive to Edwardian fashion: 'Lido' is not to be found – nothing between 'Lidrone' (a rascal) and 'Lie'. The 1976 *Supplement* to the *OED* however gives a full definition of Lido: "The name of a spit of land, a famous beach resort near Venice, now used *gen.* for: a bathing-beach or resort; a public open-air swimming pool." (The 1989 *2nd Edition* of the *OED*, Vol VIII Interval-Looie, reproduces the 1976 definition without change.) The *OED* cites references to the Venetian Lido in English as far back as the 17th century. But for Lido as an open-air pool in the UK it gives the honour of first quote in print to the *Morning Post* of 1930 July 5/4: "The safety of bathers in the Serpentine 'Lido' was raised at an inquest… yesterday."

Those inverted commas round 'Lido' indicate how new a term it was. *The Times* report of the opening of Brockwell Park Lido manages not to mention the word 'Lido' at all: it calls it a "pool" in the headline and a "swimming bath" in the text. Elsewhere, reporting on the LCC's new pools policy, its tone is dismissive: "Familiarly known as 'Lidos', the projected baths are so designated in the report of the Parks Committee…"[2.40]

And does Lido rhyme with 'Speedo' or 'Fido'? The *OED* is very firm about the pronunciation of 'lido' being as the Italians say it: the 'li' rhymes with 'fleece' and the 'do' with 'goat'. Other dictionaries permit 'li' to rhyme with 'fly' and this is perhaps now the more common usage, including by your author.

Trawling the internet, you come up with various manifestations: Lido is a river beach on the Danube at Belgrade; the 2001 debut album by Brighton-based indie-rock band, Clearlake (with a suitably municipal cover); a cabaret establishment on the Champs-Élysées, Paris; an entry-level luxury car in 1950 designed as a lower priced Lincoln; Lufthansa System's flight planning and dispatch system; a Storm Type Foundry free font; and, for computer buffs, "an input language for the attribute evaluator generator LIGA". Words it rhymes with include: credo, libido, toledo, tuxedo and escondido… Lido poems include L. E. McCullough's *Club Lido, Kansas City, 1944* ("In this crumbling black-and-grey photograph my parents smile at each other/Across a cozy corner table at the *Club Lido* in Kansas City, 1944") or Joseph Brodsky's *Venice: Lido* ("The crew, stripped to their pants – womanizers and wankers –/now that they're in the south, sun themselves by the anchors").

A very useful website for Lidos past and present (with good coverage of Brockwell Park Lido) is www.lidos.org.uk. You can also join its Lidos Yahoo Group.

Photo: Miranda Payne

LCC Parks Committee met to decide on the 17 tenders for construction of the Brockwell Park open-air pool.[2.26] The Committee chose the lowest tender, that of G Percy Trentham (GPT) Ltd, 63 New Oxford Street, London WC1, which was for £25,579.17s.8d (17s.8d = 88p approx), £353.2s.4d cheaper than the next bidder, but still much higher than the £23,000 Lambeth had been led to expect. As part of due diligence, before allowing its bid to proceed, the LCC's Solicitor had already confirmed, in winter 1935, that GPT was "in satisfactory financial standing" for constructing the Brockwell Park pool.[2.27] The highest bid was from George Wimpey & Co, and other famous names included John Mowlem and Trollope and Colls. Local builder F & FH Higgs of Herne Hill had put in a bid.

So now the LCC had a plan for a pool in Brockwell Park and a contractor to build it but Lambeth had yet to agree to pay for it.

A special meeting of Lambeth's Baths & Cemetery Committee was convened on 1936 March 31 solely to discuss the Brockwell Park open-air swimming bath. By then the LCC had made a significant concession, agreeing that Lambeth's liability would be limited to £24,150. Lambeth in turn surrendered maintenance costs and profits to the LCC, agreeing in ten minutes flat that the pegged cost of £24,150 "constitutes an appropriate and desirable settlement of the matter".[2.28]

The touch-paper was lit. The LCC first asked the Chief Parks Officer "to make a tentative approach to G Percy Trentham Ltd to ascertain the attitude of the company in regard to the tender they submitted on 19th August, 1935" – presumably to see if the passage of eight months had altered costs dramatically. On April 7, the company assured the LCC of its "willingness to carry out the work of the

construction of an open-air swimming bath at Brockwell Park for the amount of the Company's tender".[2.29] Lambeth sent letters on April 1 and May 2 confirming it would cough up its agreed £24,150. On May 12, according to the *South London Press*, the LCC was due formally to accept the tender. The paper blamed the increase from £24,150 to nearly £27,000 on "increases in the cost of labour and materials and difficulties in connection with ground levels".

The crucial appointment of JF Piggott as Clerk of Works, Class I – the eyes and ears of the LCC on the building site – was authorised on May 22, initially up to 1936 October 31, then extended to 1937 March 31 and finally to 1937 June 30 (less than a fortnight before the official opening).[2.30]

On Friday, 1936 May 29, a tiny paragraph in the *South London Press* headed 'Work Begins on Brockwell Park Swimming Pool' stated that work on the swimming bath had begun "this week": if it began at the start of the week, that would be Monday, May 25 (the Clerk of Works having been appointed on Friday May 22). "Some of the huge trees growing on the site have been uprooted and it is expected that the site will be cleared within a fortnight," the paper added – something witnessed by David Hamley (L28) (see Chapter 5). A few months later, the *South London Press* of July 7 was a little more sarcastic in its headline: 'Bathing Slips Will be O.K. at Brockwell Lido – Someone Found They Were Necessary for Sun-bathing.' According to the *SLP*, this was the first time anything but "regulation" costumes had been permitted at an LCC establishment. What was the point of building sun-bathing terraces if you couldn't strut your stuff in a slip?

By 1937 January 29, the *Brixton Free Press* was

Handtinted card of the Lido, c. 1938. Lambeth swimmers repeatedly petitioned Lambeth Council to be allowed to wear bathing slips rather than the old-fashioned costume. This group seems to have won the battle.

Photograph by W Chamberlain, from www.lambethlandmark.com. Reproduced by kind permission of Lambeth Archives.

saying "work on the bath itself [as opposed to the surrounding buildings, presumably] is almost completed". It said Brockwell Park "will now become an aquatic sports centre", as the pool was big enough for championship races, polo matches and international diving competitions.

Work on the pool seems to have gone on at an extraordinary pace. David Hamley believes this was because the builders – Irish navvies, he thinks – were paid piece-work, so the faster they laid the bricks, the better they were paid.[2.31] By 1937 April 23, the Chief Officer, Parks Department was

reporting to the LCC Parks Committee that he expected construction at Brockwell Park to be completed by May 31.[2.32] But on May 31 itself, Osmond Cattlin, Lambeth's Borough Engineer, told the MBL Baths & Cemetery Committee that the pool was only "nearing completion" and that "it was anticipated it would be ready by the 1st July next".[2.33] I haven't been able to find out the exact date the builders handed the new pool over, or when it was first filled, but it did duly open on the planned date of July 10. And the construction industry weekly, *The Builder*, had a pre-opening

ESCAPE In 1989 I remember going for a swim after a close friend had died. After his funeral I came back and had a swim. It was wonderful to have a swim after the tense time – **Andreas Demetriou (L18)**

I liked Brockwell because… it was very big and you didn't feel hemmed in by other people – **Jacqui Gilbert (L25)**

Knowing it's there makes living in the city bearable, if not excellent! **(S96)**

Opportunity to escape noise, traffic, pollution, litter, violence **(S639)**

At the 1963 LCC Swimming Championships Finals at Brockwell Park Lido, July 13, where 13 new records were set. Photographer Ron Chapman. Reproduced by kind permission of London Metropolitan Archives.

photo of a filled pool in its commemorative report of 1937 July 16.

Skirmishing between Metropolitan Borough of Lambeth and the LCC continued right up to the end almost. At a full MBL Council meeting on 1937 March 24, Councillor H Williman raised a question about the notice board in the Park relating to the new open-air bath, which mentioned the LCC but not MBL. The Councillor "considered that, as the Borough Council provided £24,000 of the capital money, such notice board should give publicity to this fact".[234]

A more serious matter came at the last hurdle. At the same meeting where Engineer Osmond Cattlin

told the Baths & Cemetery Committee that the pool was "nearing completion" he let drop the bombshell that "the appropriate Committee of the LCC had decided not to hold an official opening ceremony". The B&CC concluded that an official opening ceremony *should* be held – and under the auspices of the MBL "and His Worship the Mayor consented to perform such ceremony". Once the LCC had been informed of this decision, it speedily informed Lambeth that its Engineer was labouring under a misapprehension and that the LCC did indeed intend to hold such a ceremony, which, however, it was "willing" for the Mayor of Lambeth to perform.[235]

That prickly issue dealt with, the way was clear for the celebration of a great civic achievement. On June 25, the Clerk of the LCC gave an outline to the Parks Committee "of an appropriate form of ceremony on 10th July" – so by that late June date the building must have been in a fit state to receive dignitaries.

For dignitaries there were to be, and in abundance. A canopied dais was to be built poolside "for those taking a leading part" but – with typical English class differentiation – "uncovered seating for a general company of about 400 members and guests". There was to be amplification – and a band from the London Fire Brigade, which presumably didn't need it. And the opening ceremony was to be followed by an equal-opportunity aquatic display "by students of the Borough Polytechnic Boys School and the Mary Datchelor Girls' School". The bath cafeteria was to earn its spurs with "the supply of refreshments". A total expenditure "not exceeding £55 (£2300 today)" was sanctioned.[2.36]

Ahead of the opening, the local press waxed lyrical. 'Rippling River' was the headline in the *Brixton Free Press* on July 9, the day before the opening, explaining that "a feature of the pool is a constant surface current, which gives the appearance of a rippling river and removes all floating matter" – thanks to the unromantically named but innovative "scum trough" at the deep end.

The opening ceremony was scheduled to start at 3pm on Saturday, 1937 July 10. As so often at this period, the LCC had printed both a descriptive leaflet of the 'New Open-Air Swimming Bath' – not 'Pool' or 'Lido' – and a detailed 'Order of Proceedings' for the actual ceremony.[2.37]

Even the august *Times* covered the opening, one of only three times it included the Lido in its authoritative pages up to 1985. Its major story was 'More Swimming Baths – Chain of Open-Air Pools – LCC's £150,000 [£6.3 million today] Scheme', an account of the LLC's major policy shift on Lidos (illustrated by a map of 14 existing and 5 proposed 'swimming baths' across London), due for discussion the next day. But there was a small paragraph at the end, headed 'Brockwell Park Pool', which completely avoided using the L word – Lido, presumably too vulgar a neologism for the *Times*: "The Mayor of Lambeth… inaugurated on Saturday an open-air swimming bath in Brockwell Park, SE… Civic authorities representing neighbouring boroughs attended the opening ceremony. Provision has been made for ambulance and café services." The paper of record inaccurately stated that the bath "has been provided by the LCC at a cost of £26,000" – presumably to the chagrin of the Metropolitan Borough of Lambeth, which actually had furnished the money.

On July 16, the *Brixton Free Press*'s full and lively account of the July 10 opening had four headlines: 'London's Newest Lido – Lambeth's Mayor Throws Girl in to open Bath at Brockwell Park – Councillor Surprises Colleagues and Enjoys a Swim – Happy Example of Co-operation.' The photo illustrating the story was captioned: 'The Mayor with a bevy of bathing belles at the opening of the swimming pool.'

The fourth and smallest headline, 'Happy Example of Co-operation' picked up on allusions, perhaps through gritted teeth, in speeches by both the LCC Parks Committee Chair, Ruth Dalton, and Lambeth's Mayor EA Mills JP to the effect that the Lido "showed what could be done by friendly co-operation between two local authorities". Mrs

Dalton introduced the Mayor, the Mayor made a long speech, detailing the history of the pool's creation and thanking its creators. He then declared the bath open, at which a fanfare sounded. Votes of thanks were moved to park staff and LCC staff; in her final words, Mrs Dalton even thanked the boys and girl swimmers who had come to entertain them. WF Marchant, LCC Member for Norwood said he "cherished a feeling for the old lake" but that the new bath "was quite beyond his dreams".

Symbolic of the true nature of their "harmonious" relationship, though the Mayor of Lambeth actually opened the bath, the LCC's Ruth Dalton presided over the day and got the last word. Well, the last official word. Because the Mayor then proceeded to the poolside where, with the help of an attendant, he "threw the first swimmer into the bath – a girl from Mary Datchelor Girls' School. She sent up a great splash and the Mayor caught best part of it – and laughed heartily."

That fifteen-year-old schoolgirl was Thelma Phelps (L47), now 85 and a retired doctor. She remembers July 10 as "a nice day and of course the mayor was there".

Dr Phelps was part of the local Mary Datchelor School swimming team that took part in the Lido's opening ceremony, the only one of our interviewees to do so. The school had its own indoor pool and reached a high standard of swimming. At the Lido, "we gave a display of swimming, to music, and a display of diving", she said. At the opening day she remembers "the impressive diving boards" and the fountain at the shallow end.

On the actual opening Saturday, 1937 July 10, "we were taken down in a crocodile, by the PT mistress, a Miss Coggan", she said. "We did the

display which was quite complicated and quite impressive, making figures floating. And then we did the diving and I remember the press said that wasn't good enough, they wanted something more spectacular. We were all hanging around and one came up to me and said, 'You look a nice girl. We're going to ask the Mayor to throw you in,' which is what happened. I thought, I've never been told I was a nice girl before! At 15… well I suppose I was. The Mayor took the top half of me and the press chap took the feet [not the "attendant" mentioned in the press] and did '1, 2, 3' and in I went and lots of photographs."

Dr Phelps said she "didn't mind being thrown in". But that attitude wasn't shared by Miss Coggan: "She was not very well pleased. It was not her idea of how to open a pool, she didn't like her girls being shown up in that way. She didn't have words but she looked…"

A photo was taken of the swimming team and the Mayor: "And he was a big well-built man and he wore his chain. I heard he remarked at some kind of function later he was glad it wasn't throwing another heavy girl in the pool. I was only eight stone, I wasn't very pleased about that."

The Mary Datchelor girls and the Polytechnic boys also had a relay race, which the boys won, according to the the *Brixton Free Press* report. Middle-aged Lambeth Councillor Wilkinson also plunged in, given a hearty 'hand' by colleagues. Few of the general public responded to a mike invitation to enjoy a swim, not having brought swimming costumes. But Brockwell Park Lido was well and truly launched on the world.

Timeline 2: Towards the Lido: The 1920s–1930s campaign for open-air bathing in Lambeth

1923 Motion before LCC to use unemployed labour in 'construction of open-air bath': proposal rejected 1928 MBL writes to LCC, asking it to extend facilities at lake and introduce mixed bathing: proposal rejected 1929 MBL again writes to LCC, stressing health benefits of open-air baths in parks; LCC unenthusiastic 1933 LCC writes to MBL, warning of insanitary conditions at lake; offered to allocate site for modern open-air bath near Rosendale Road, cost £12,000 1934 **JANUARY** MBL formally accepts proposal for new pool, but asks LCC to extend it to include more modern facilities **JULY 3** LCC writes to MBL offering new site for bigger pool by Dulwich Road **JULY 27** LCC Parks Committee drives to Brockwell Park for a site visit **AUGUST** Estimate for building Lido doubles to £23,000 1935 **JANUARY** MBL accepts Dulwich Road site **APRIL** LCC asks for tenders to build Lido. Lake definitively shut to bathers **SEPTEMBER** Parks Committee chair opens 17 sealed tenders. 1936 **MARCH 14** LCC picks lowest tender, G Percy Trentham Ltd's, for £25,000 **MARCH 31** MBL confirms it will pay for new Lido **APRIL 7** G Percy Trentham Ltd confirms its price **MAY 22** Work starts on preparing ground 1937 **APRIL** Parks Officer reports Lido work expected to be completed by May 31 **SATURDAY, JULY 10, 3PM** Ceremonial Opening of Brockwell Park Lido by Mayor of Lambeth

An iconic image of the post-war Lido – the octagonal 'aerator' fountain at the shallow
end, 1948. Its function was to oxygenate the water, recycling it back to the main pool.
Several of our interviewees said that the fountain was out of bounds in their time, strictly
monitored by staff.

Chapter 3

1937–1993, from Opening to Closing

'The clock above the door. The tannoy system, diving boards, the water chutes, the fountain and I can still see Cyril Fry standing behind his counter dishing out his bits and pieces.' – Marlene Devaney

It is difficult to capture what a Lido meant in 1937 Britain. Right after all the official flim-flam of the opening ceremony, Brockwell Park's started to fulfil its function: the *Brixton Free Press* reported that "later in the day some splashed about in London's latest Lido", while on the following day, a Sunday, "it was well patronised".[3.1] Different eras, different cultures, of course, but Brockwell Park Lido in 1937 represented an extraordinary funnelling of energy and potential for South London – for the hardy all-round swimmers graduating from the lake (and still getting their early morning swims for free); for children larking about or getting their first swimming lessons there; for athletes competing for prizes and money. On some days, the Lido was so crowded that a shift system would operate, with coloured discs to indicate your time slot.

Daniel Patrick Willoughby (L63), born 1924, remembers a fenced football pitch on the Lido site – the local team was called the Effra (after the local underground 'lost' river) – and that local people were excited about it being a Lido. For him, "it was the best Lido in Great Britain because it had everything". No other Lido in London had the sunbathing space, he says. It was built with a cafeteria run by a Mr Fry – kids would grab the chance to make deliveries to him to get in free.

The Lido would close at lunch. Local lads would climb the wall at night, but he'd go in for a swim before supper.

"I would come home from work. I was working in Battersea in a printing firm and I would take swimming trunks in the morning and tell my aunt that I would have a swim and don't do the beans on toast too early and [I would] have a swim. It was a lovely swim. You see what happened during the war – such as the swimming pool was a marvellous thing for people – for people didn't have a big choice of entertainment so they made it their entertainment and the pool, the Lido, was terrific to spend a half-hour or hour in and then go home – in the summer, not in the winter sadly.

"There was a drowning – a death where a chap was swimming under or near the high diver and somebody jumped off the high diver not looking to see what was below and he hit the swimmer and he drowned.

"Sport is not popular today. I associate the pool with all sport. Brockwell Park had 12 football pitches in those days because I played on no. 12 and today you have two and they are very rarely used and the Lido has to go in that category: that people were like that in those days because you made your own pleasure and swimming was like that."

A 1937 image of the Lido, perhaps pre-opening. It shows the fence that divided spectators from swimmers, who each had separate entrances and toilets. The Lido was designed for spectacle, to host galas and races. In the 1930s what differentiated a Lido from a simple bathing pool was the provision of extra facilities such as a spectator terrace, sunbathing area and café.

Photographer unknown. Reproduced by kind permission of London Metropolitan Archives.

Janet Smith is very good on the combination of national and international factors that meant Lidos really caught the spirit of their age.[32] First, Lidos were classless (unlike the covered pools at the time which had 1st and 2nd classes) and, unlike the lakes, mixed-sex. Thanks to the writings of Swiss doctor Auguste Rollier, the alleged health benefits of sun-bathing ('heliotherapy') were widely broadcast and where better for one to get the sun at home than a Lido? Coco Chanel's promotion of tanning lotions garnered the *fashionistas*. The year after Brockwell Park Lido opened, the *Holidays with Pay Act* of 1938 gave all workers a minimum one week's paid holiday between May and October. Sometimes simple jealousy, such as that of fitness-obsessed Nazi Germany's sporting prowess (showcased in 1936 at the Berlin Olympics) worked its way into the British soul. There was a similar trajectory in the US, with a movement from public baths for the poor at the start of the 20th century to sexy, classless open air pools in the 1930s (not called 'lidos', though – that remained a British quirk).[33]

LCC politicians were keenly alive to the *zeitgeist*. In 1935, the Parks Committee unusually announced a three-year programme of special works (as

34

opposed to the more normal annual estimates) to build seven new baths after Victoria Park and Brockwell Park.[3.4] And on June 25, only a few weeks before Brockwell Park Lido opened, the LCC Parks Committee produced a major report on the desirability of lidos in general and of the LCC building them "without delay", as the Committee was "convinced" there was "a widespread demand" for them – a report that was endorsed by the full Council on July 13, three days after Brockwell Park Lido opened.[3.5] In LCC elections earlier that year, Labour retained power, with a gain of six seats. LCC Labour leader Herbert Morrison had made Lidos part of his electoral programme: "In March [1937] I promised the people of London that the new LCC would make London a City of Lidos. Here we are."[3.6]

According to the *Times'* July 12 preview of the LCC July 13 discussion, construction costs for the new chain of Lidos in London were to be offset by "revenue for charges to be made for mixed bathing". An idyllic picture was painted by Parks Committee chair Ruth Dalton (who had represented the LCC at the opening of the Lido): "The most modern purifying plant would be installed… There would be sunbathing terraces, cafés providing refreshments indoors, and, at the larger baths, room for spectators. Flower beds near the water and a vista of trees in the background would make a lovely setting for happy summer days" – nothing if not a description of Brockwell Park Lido…

The Parks Committee definition of 'lido' was: "open-air swimming baths with the added amenities of sun-bathing areas, cafés and other facilities which will make them attractive places of healthy public resort" – as good a definition as any, and, incidentally, all things the Metropolitan Borough of Lambeth had been banging on about

since 1929, a subtle illustration that the relationship between centre and periphery was occasionally two-way.

It was decided to build five more Lidos – Charlton, Parliament Hill, Battersea, Ladywell and Clissold – in a period of three years. The coming war killed off the grand scheme, with only the first two being built. But a new Lido just for children was even opened at Mary Harmsworth Park (near the Imperial War Museum) in 1938.[3.7] Lido mania reached north of Edinburgh: the Stonehaven sea-water, Olympic-sized, Art Deco pool was first opened by local public subscription in June 1934, and flourishes yet.[3.8]

For Joan Hunt (L34), a schoolgirl before the war, galas at the Lido were an opportunity to win prizes in cash and in kind: "If your parents don't have much money and you can swim and you win races, then you get a free pass. You can imagine I made such an effort. I had that pass for three years and if you won prizes in the gala they used to give us money to buy what you like. I had a heyday absolutely." Jean Phelps (L48) recalls the crowds being so great that a shift system operated: "Sessions were in force when the pool was cleared and space created for others to have a swim." She conquered her fear of deep water by inching along "the sections of ribbed stones round the edge of the pool (they are still there)" until she came to a point when her feet no longer touched the bottom: "I shall never forget the excitement and sense of achievement."

David Hamley (L28) remembers exactly how the shift system was done: "People would come for miles only to be allowed in for an hour because you had a different coloured disc and the man would come out of his little [observation] booth where the clock was and he would come out and say, 'All those with

FAMILY-FRIENDLY I visit from time to time and bring the kids down. They are old enough to go on their own now. I usually just sit back and let them enjoy it. The atmosphere is nice. You will see groups – little groups of people in corners, family groups like. They're going in the water, having their sandwiches, listening to music, reading, anything – sunbathing. Nice to see in the inner city, so much beach life. – **Cheryl Gillespie (L70)**

Safe for children (**S38**)

It's local, a community space where my children and I meet friends and schoolmates (**S123**)

It is a friendly and safe place to take the whole family. And have a great time (**S243**)

Photograph courtesy of Whippersnappers

yellow discs – to the changing rooms, please'."

At the end of the first year of operation, MBL petitioned the LCC to move one of the women-only days from Thursday. Thursday (along with Wednesday) was an early closing day in Lambeth and MBL wanted it to be free for mixed bathing, although it recognised "the need for one day being set apart for women bathers".[3.9] The LCC agreed.[3.10] Councillor James, who raised the matter, made the more general point that the allocation of times between men (82.75hrs per week) and women (55hrs) was unfair. However, local women seemed to have relished their women only morning. In 1938 May, the LCC discontinued a London-wide experiment of women-only mornings because of low take-up, except at Brockwell Lido, where attendance was a respectable average of 90 women a day.[3.11]

1938 also saw a significant development in Lido governance. The LCC finally decided in July that it had had enough of negotiating with local boroughs over Lidos. It felt it was "desirable… that there should be a uniform system of administration of the baths… [and] advisable for the Council to take full responsibility for the cost of maintenance and baths". It would also assume full responsibility for improvement and enlargement of baths, but – alas, poor Lambeth – "not in any case reimburse any past capital expenditure". The new regime was backdated to begin 1938 April 1.[3.12] MBL surrendered to the inevitable and "received" the decision.[3.13]

At the same 1938 May meeting that reported on the women-only mornings experiment, there was a premonition of war: the LCC stated "it has no objection… to the ear-marking by the Home Office of LCC Lidos for use as first-aid posts or clearing stations during hostile air raids". The international situation of 1939 had an impact even on humble lidos. In February, a joint report from the Fire Brigade & Main Drainage and the Parks Committees of the LCC agreed that Brockwell Park Lido, like others, should be available to the Fire Brigade for emergency water supplies. As the Lido was a little way from the Dulwich Road, expenditure was authorised for permanent suction pipes to be fitted to the Lido and taken to the Park boundary.[3.14]

How comforting it was amidst the alarums of imminent war that the clothing police of the Amateur Swimming Association found time to alert Lambeth's Baths & Cemetery Committee about correct swimwear for competitive events. Males "shall wear" either the full costume (ie one that covered the chest), with drawers or slips underneath or (great concession), "if sanctioned by the bath authority concerned", swimming trunks with drawers or slips underneath. Females "shall wear" costumes "of one piece devoid of open work excepting at the back". All costumes and trunks were to be non-transparent.[3.15] Transparent swimwear in 1939? The mind boggles. Lambeth's stroppy swimmers made "repeated requests" to be allowed to wear swimming trunks on mixed bathing days and Baths & Cemetery gave its blessing.[3.16] The Amateur Swimming Association's current librarian Wendy Coles confirms[3.17] that at the time competitors' costumes were made of silk with a Union Jack badge. Slips (underwear) were required "because silk is clingy and semi-transparent".

There were even those who harked back to the naturist days of the lake. Jeffrey Rumble in *A Brockwell Boy* claims there was occasional nudity in the Lido: "It was not unknown for some of the lads to take the plunge nude… this was quite contrary to the published rules, which required gentlemen to wear slips under their costumes."[3.18] This was doubtless because there were still daily men-only sessions until 9.45am. Thursdays were women-only and both Monday and Friday were men-only, which left weekends and Tuesday/Wednesday for mixed bathing – hardly a sexual revolution.[3.19]

Another LCC Committee, Education, brought an optimistic note to the dark year of 1939. Responding to a request from the London & Middlesex Area Committee of the National Fitness Council, it agreed to a one-year experiment of "classes in physical training, including swimming instruction" at three Lidos: Brockwell Park, Parliament Hill Fields and Victoria Park. Six temporary instructors, with equal pay for women and men of 100s (£5) per week, were to provide 13 weeks of instruction over the summer of 1939.[3.20] Although the Second World War disrupted these lessons, they were a strong feature of the post-War Lido and another example that progress is not always sustained: I am not aware of any local authority-sponsored instruction in the Lido over the past dozen years.

The cataclysm of war broke in the UK on 1939 September 3. Astonishingly early, given all that was going on, the LCC's Emergency Committee – into

BEACH I do remember those chaps, polished conkers – men in their sixties who used to swim at Brockwell Lido. – **Ruth Thompson (L56)**

Bring more of the park inside so that it's more green… palm trees… beachify it, tropicalise it… a sand effect kind of flooring… not real sand… to encourage people to bring their children… maybe a waterfall… some sort of slide… log seats… stone seats… pebbles… a soft rock in the pool that children could climb up on… – **Marcia Cameron (L10)**

which the pre-War Committees like Parks had been subsumed – took a firm decision of principle on September 19: "We have given authority that, until further order, games and other similar facilities and amenities in the Council's parks and open spaces should be allowed to continue."[3.21]

Proof of this commitment to sporting business as usual, the LCC decided, 1940 April 30, to open all its Lidos for the 1940 season.[3.22] At the same time it swept away, due to pressure of war (but presented, as usual, as "an experiment"), 50 years of sex segregation and discrimination in bathing provision: "In view of the desirability of providing additional facilities for women bathers and the probable difficulty of obtaining male attendants with life-saving qualifications, mixed bathing will be permitted… at all times." As the 1939 Lambeth kerfuffle over male swimming trunks showed, the bastion was already being undermined, but this decision blew it sky high.

The LCC managed against great odds to maintain a swimming season at its Lidos in each year of the war: 1941,[3.23] 1942,[3.24] 1943,[3.25] 1944[3.26] and 1945.[3.27] As usual, Lidos opened for early morning swims and shut "at 9pm or sunset", whichever was earlier.[3.28]

In 1942, the LCC allowed Brockwell Park Lido to be reserved for part of a Saturday "for an aquatic sports meeting organised primarily for members of the regiments of Guards".[3.29]

1942 also saw a Government initiative called 'Holidays at Home', an attempt to get people to enjoy themselves without travelling away from their locality and thus saving transport costs. The LCC subsidised a huge range of events, sporting and cultural, in its parks as part of 'Holidays at Home' It built an open air theatre at Brockwell Park, replacing

the Victorian bandstand, and this hosted opera, ballet and musicals.[3.30] At Brockwell Park and Parliament Hill Fields Lidos, swimming galas were organised in 1942,[3.31] with admission charges and programme sales helping defray the costs. The ability to hold galas was designed into the DNA of Brockwell Park Lido, of course – and was a pattern that was to continue throughout and after the war, right up to the 1960s as a major feature of those two Lidos' existence.

The two galas next year, 1943, proved "very popular, with attendances which were an improvement on those of last year".[3.32] The Mayor of Lambeth opened the Brockwell Park gala and the Lady Mayoress distributed medals and prizes. All looked set fair for even better galas north and south of the Thames in 1944, but on 1944 July 13 a flying bomb destroyed Brockwell Park's Open Air Theatre – and both projected swimming galas were "abandoned owing to the prevailing situation and the lack of entries".[3.33]

For Elsie Turner, "our favourite place was Brockwell Park". It had "a lovely swimming pool open to the sky. In the pool there was a snack bar, and we used to lay on our towels by the edge of the pool or sit at one of the tables.

"In the swimming pool they had a big thing shaped like a jelly with water cascading down, which you could climb on. Also there were slides and diving boards at the deep end." One day Elsie was walking to Brockwell Park to go swimming when a "Buzz Bomb" came flying overhead. All of a sudden the buzzing stopped, which meant that it would start to fall. She dashed into a nearby house for protection, only to find a deaf old lady in bed. Told a buzz bomb might be imminent, the old lady simply went under her bed-clothes. "I lay down on

HAVEN/OASIS The fact that it is actually enclosed makes it a safe haven ...it's also very open so it's a kind of a contradiction really... – **Theresa Hoare (L31)**

And then when I was in the water lying on my back it was a sort of floating – it was a lovely free feeling of looking up at the sky and seeing all the greenery around the trees. It was sort of heavenly. – **Catherine Steinger (L54)**

It is a refreshing thing for the mind when the weather is good. – **Daniel Patrick Willoughby (L63)**

A haven, the blueness, the old-fashioned quality of the place (S16)

the floor and waited, but the bomb fell far away."[3.34]

In 1945, the final year of war, "it was found possible to hold two galas" at Brockwell Park and Parliament Hill Fields but school entries proved difficult to find "as during the war years swimming has not been featured in the school curriculum to the same extent as in normal times". Although the number of entries was not large, therefore, the galas were deemed a success, "the area available for spectators being filled to capacity on both occasions".[3.35]

A constant refrain during the war was the difficulty in obtaining suitable staff[3.36] – men would be called up to fight, while women were drafted into all sorts of work more important than running a lido. Even the long tradition of all-year-round swimming seems to have suffered, with the Lido closed in December both in 1943[3.37] and 1944, due to lack of patrons.[3.38]

Asked about lifeguards during the war, Daniel Patrick Willoughby (L63) said: "You wouldn't have noticed. Things were haphazard. There was a lack of human beings during the war. Hundreds and thousands of people left during the war because of the bombings."

History is full of 'what ifs'. One could speculate what might have happened to the fledgling Lido had war not come in 1939. Against the background of what was going on in the world at the time, the vicissitudes of a swimming pool (including bomb damage to it) truly amount to very little.

But the point is, the Lido did matter, at the time – season after season, from 1940–45, the LCC opened it, people swam there and children learned to swim in it. Galas took place, perhaps fires on Dulwich Road were put out with Lido water – and presumably somehow some solace in a dreadful

world was found. Former Brixton Market stallholder Irene Cowell (L67), for instance, used to work during the war in Brixton Town Hall, "so on my way to work every morning, I used to go into the Lido for a morning swim. It was only a 15-minute walk for me from home to the Lido, but I am not saying how my hair looked when I arrived in my office, certainly not curly, for the swimming caps rarely kept all the water out". Now in her 80s she still takes her grandchildren to the Park and to the Lido.

The post-war era began – and the first decade of the Lido's existence concluded – with a decision that the summer season in LCC Lidos would begin on 1946 April 18, "subject to sufficient qualified staff being available".[3.39] And the wartime initiative was resumed, with swimming galas at Brockwell Park on July 20 and Parliament Hill Fields on September 7, "because galas have a popular appeal".[3.40]

The Brockwell Park gala was organised in association with "the Brockwell Park Swimming Club" (if this is the same as the 1908 body (*see Chapter 1*), what astonishing longevity – and what became of it?). The Parliament Hill Fields gala was organised in association with "the Highgate Life Buoys" (!). Entries and attendances were said to be good "and the Bathing Beauty Contest at Parliament Hill Fields judged by Tommy Handley [a popular comedian] was very successful".[3.41]

The LCC this year instituted London-wide championships in athletics and bowls.[3.42]

By the next year, 1947, normal peacetime activities returned, with the Parks Committee voting £600 – £14,400 today – for chlorination plant at Brockwell Park and Tooting Bec Lidos. Swimming lessons were re-instituted by the LCC Education Committee, with instructors getting equal pay of 150s (£7.50, £180 today, compared with pre-war £5)

PEACE There is just this peacefulness within the Lido which is strange because usually it is hundreds of people splashing around in the pool. Just the calmness of it – that is why it is an attractive venue to have a wedding or a birthday party. – **Douglas Whitton (L60)**

Peace and tranquillity on an early weekend morning (**S31**)

The peace and quiet, away from the traffic (**S47**)

Sanctuary. Peace. My favourite place (**S56**)

The tranquillity, the greenery around the walls, being able to sunbathe topless (**S66**)

Photo: Miranda Payne

for a six-day, five-hour-a-day week for free physical training and swimming instruction at Brockwell Park, Parliament Hill, Victoria Park and Charlton Lidos.[343] Perhaps to help pay for this, spectator fees were doubled, to 2d ('tuppence', less than 1p) for children and 4d ('fourpence', about 1½p, 36p today) for adults.[344]

But the most significant Lido-related decision the LCC took in 1947 was to expand the London-wide athletics and bowls championships begun in 1946 to include tennis and swimming – perhaps partly because of the success of the 1946 (and wartime) galas. Having taken the decision in February to go ahead, the Parks Committee circularised the secretaries of 80 lawn tennis and

100 swimming clubs in the London area, asking for their co-operation in setting up the new championships.[345]

It was all done with expedition. Area swimming heats were held: south of the river, at Brockwell Park Lido on June 7 and north of the river, at Parliament Hill Fields Lido on June 21, with the finals of the first 'County of London (LCC) Swimming Championships' taking place at Parliament Hill on 1947 July 12. In addition to the competitions, a water polo exhibition was held and the significance of the new event was underlined by the Leader of the LCC, Lord Latham, giving out the swimming prizes. Parks Committee reported to the full LCC that the new swimming championships "proved very popular".[346]

1959 and a lady felt naked without white gloves… There were a record 594 competitors at the LCC swimming championships this year, with 14 records broken. Fine weather, with 651 spectators at Brockwell Park Lido for the finals, July 18.

Photographer Ron Chapman. Reproduced by kind permission of London Metropolitan Archives.

For 22 years, from 1947–1968, the same pattern was followed, with preliminary heats north and south of the Thames at Parliament Hill and Brockwell Park respectively and the finals alternating between the two venues (it was Brockwell Park's turn to host the finals in 1948 and then 1950, 1952, 1954, 1955, 1957, 1959, 1961, 1963).

The Lido was purpose-built to house spectacles like these so in a way these 22 championship seasons represent glory years for Brockwell Park Lido. In fact, one of the few appearances of the Lido in the London *Times* is a fine photo of a woman diver at the 1963 Championships: "Miss F Cramp [strange name for a swimmer], aged 16, who retained her County of London Girls diving championship at Brockwell Park Lido yesterday. She is the All-England schools' junior diving champion, and is in the British team for the European diving contests in Leipzig next week."[3.47] Appendix 2 gives the details of this era and it is both a story of increasing prestige and success – growing competitor numbers and spectators, breaking of records, participation by top athletes, including Olympians – and an illustration of how a strategic authority like the LCC or GLC can use its critical mass to stage events of national importance.

It would be easy to say the transition from LCC to GLC was the death knell for championships in the Lido, but the answer at the time was more prosaic and also inherent in the nature of a Lido. Three years of simple bad weather from 1966–68 combined with the arrival of superb indoor facilities at Crystal Palace to kibosh the Lidos' role in the Championships.

In retrospect, this was a near-fatal blow. Without the prestige of such an annual event, such spectacle, the Lido became, to coin a phrase, a bit of a backwater. At the beginning of the decade, the

Marlene Devaney: The Lido in the 1950s

Marlene Devaney, née Smith (L65), born 1948, was the daughter of the head keeper of Brockwell Park – and "couldn't get away with anything because we were so well known that if we did anything wrong Dad would hear about it" – and lived there until she left to get married in 1969. Her memories of the Lido of her childhood in the 1950s are detailed and clear. She learnt to swim in the Lido, "under the watchful eye of 'Goody', otherwise known as Mrs Goodwin, always in a white overall with her cossie on underneath, not that anyone ever saw it". And she has poignant memories of Cyril Fry, who ran the café, rain or shine.

On a Saturday or Sunday and during the holidays the queue to get into the Lido "would go right up to the bowling green and then meander around to the tennis court bothy or go around the other way".

Like Graham Gower (L27), she remembers the changing rooms as "cold – except if the sun was shining, it just took the chill off. So the doors always banged as we went in there. There was nothing quiet about them, they always banged as we went in there. We'd get in there, get changed quickly and go and get a basket; they didn't have lockers. You'd take your towel outside with you but if you were really daring you'd take your clothes outside with you as well but so be it on your head if you did that.

"If we did not go through the foot pool the staff would call you back and say 'in there' and it was only cold water but oh to try and nip out between the staff catching you and going through that pool."

Swimmers and spectators were issued with different coloured tickets, but if a spectator tried to cheat and get a swim, "if the staff weren't happy they would come round and check your ticket. If you had the wrong colour ticket you would be asked to pay the extra money or if you refused you were kicked out."

The Lido closed for lunch, with morning session 9–1 and afternoon session from 2 to closing time, "so you really had your money's worth".

Parents trusted children to the Lido unsupervised: "People in the area knew that the staff down there were good, especially with the youngsters, it wasn't a major problem but they did watch an awful lot if anyone came into the pool that they were not happy with. They were very alert with it."

But Mrs Goodwin was "the head pool lady, like a life guard". She was a Lido fixture for Marlene: "I can't think of a time when Goody was not there. She was there when I was little and she was there when I left the park. I will never forget the white overall and the white plimsolls. She used to have her swimming costume on underneath her overall and that is what the staff at that time did – you never saw them walking around in their swimming costumes. The overalls were there as their uniforms. But I am thinking at that time there was still that decorum of modesty and when you saw a uniform you knew where they were in the pool so you couldn't get up to anything. They would stand under the clock there where people came in and their eyes were everywhere."

She said the café was "basic, very, very basic. A counter that was so high that you could just about see what you were getting. Cyril used to have someone work down there for him during the week in the summer but Cyril would come down at the weekend and do it himself or he would help but there was hot Bovril, bread rolls, buttered rolls, bread and butter, sweets, and cakes, hot Bovril, tea and coffee. It was more tea, then the coffee crept in. There were a few tables in there with chairs which were metal, rickety and blue, grey and blue depending on when they were painted. Sometimes there would be a few chairs and seats outside the café so that you could sit there but nine times out of ten you'd walk along – and we did not have so much paper cups but more china cups so you had to take your cup back. You did NOT leave Cyril's cups – Mr Fry's cups – in the areas because you would get your ears bashed. That was very basic and the floor was always very slippery with everyone walking in there when they were dripping wet, a towel wrapped around your shoulders and you'd stand there shivering so you'd go in there and get your hot Bovril. It wasn't very expensive, I think maybe it was only a penny or tuppence a cup. At that time it was really good. But if you went down there and the money was a bit short you would obviously take your own picnic."

And the weather? "Oh gosh – it was always sunny. If it would come over cloudy we would just dive in the café until it would stop raining, gather all of our stuff up. Some times Cyril would get a lot of trade out of it but other times we would all stand in there waiting for it to stop raining and no one would buy anything so he would get quite frustrated with us.

"The fountain – we were never allowed to get into it. We were told not to get into it. We were shouted at if we got into it but over the years you climbed into it because the water would come gushing out and somebody would try to sit on the very top tier to stop it coming out. But because the days were so hot you would sit in there. There was an accident one year and I'm not sure of the whys and wherefores but not long after that they put small railings up on it. They were only about 2ft high to my mind but you were not then supposed to go in there and eventually the fountain was turned off. It was regarded as dangerous. We had the water chutes on the side of the pool and we had the diving boards. It was good for all ages. But I suppose over the years when people went a bit silly on the diving boards doing bombings and things like that they started banging their heads on the bottom of the pool. I had my mouth smacked a few times on the side of the pool after jumping off the bouncy board."

She said the diving boards were there all the years that she was there and she missed them and a lot besides: "I felt that there was such a lot missing. It had taken away the character of the Lido: The clock above the door. The tannoy system, diving boards, the water chutes, the fountain and I can still see Cyril Fry standing behind his counter dishing out his bits and pieces. I can see that the character has gone and that is what I miss when I go there."

Interviewed by Mary Hill

Report of the Committee on Sport and the Community, chaired by Sir John Wolfenden, had said (Paragraph 79): "More swimming baths are urgently needed. As a general rule this provision should be indoor."[3.48] So the writing was already on the wall.

When weather is fine, a Lido is a wonderful place to be and when it is not, not. When the fair-weather friends go, Lidos are vulnerable and need special friends… I guess this tension will surround open-air pools in this country for a long time.

Apart from the championships, the regular life of the Lido went on. In 1949, Councillor Scott asked Parks Committee chair Ruth Dalton – who had taken part in the 1937 July 10 opening ceremony – if she were aware "of the condition of the Brockwell Park baths" and would she take "immediate steps" to repair war damage? Mrs Dalton's replies were crisp and not very forthcoming: "Temporary repairs to war damage at Brockwell Park Lido have enabled it to be heavily used by the public during the past summer" and "as soon as work of higher priority… has been attended to, permanent repairs will be carried out at the Lido".[3.49] Higher priorities lasted some time: an allocation of £9319 (£158,000 today) to Grace & Marsh Ltd, for "war damage repairs, Brockwell Park Lido" wasn't reported till 1952.[3.50] The following year, £2020 was voted for "mudding out Brockwell Park lake".

Artist Catherine Steinger (L54), born 1933, would make a day of it for herself and her children in the 1950s and provide accordingly: "I would make all the sandwiches in the kitchen at home and put them in my wicker shopping basket. It was usually boiled eggs and tomato sandwiches and a few extra tomatoes and fruit of course and the usual fish paste sandwiches in those days and juice and we used to just walk up the park and straight to the Lido and of course I would take a tea cloth and napkins cause I always liked to do things nice."

Times changed another key element of the original Lido vision in 1958, when the LCC abolished separate arrangements for spectators, "to economise with staff, by dispensing with separate entrances and enclosures for spectators".[3.51] All adults at all LCC Lidos had henceforth to pay the full entrance fee of 9d (3.75p) (or 1s (5p, 70p today) on weekends/bank holidays), "whether they wish to bathe or only to watch".

Small changes went on all the time. In 1960, £1833 was spent "re-laying paving in Brockwell Park Lido and repairing drainage channels".[3.52] In 1961, another swing of the 'what do we do with our clothes?' pendulum saw baskets for clothes replaced by lockers.[3.53]

Jacqui Gilbert (L25) described the pool as being "very quiet" in the 1950s. She taught at Kingsdale School from 1959 to 1961 and swam at the Lido "when the weather was good". She said, "It was still very much a deserted place". While Pat Challen (L68) said: "I have some lovely memories of days we spent as a family in Brockwell Park and the Lido about 40 years ago [ie in the 1960s]. My daughter spent almost every weekend in the Lido, then after a good swim would enjoy a glass of fizzy lemonade from the White House."

Roddy Gray (L66), youth worker at the Vassall Road Community Centre, recalled going to the Lido just after he came to England from Jamaica in 1966. He went swimming there for the first time in England, and was used to swimming in the river in Jamaica. He said, "I jumped in and thought, 'Oh, My God I'm going to die' – I just couldn't believe how cold the water was – it was freezing! We used to

'The Brockwell Icicles' were a famous Lido club of the post-war period. To join, you had to break the ice on a winter's day and swim. Caroline Russell, c1960, displays her badge of admission to the club.

Photo courtesy of Caroline Russell.

play football on the pitch, then go swimming in the pool afterwards... It was for everybody... and I couldn't believe how deep it was, at the deep end... so I used to keep to the shallow end." But he added, "It was a nice place to cool off."

A famous Lido club, the Brockwell Icicles, made its way into the minutes of the GLC in 1968, when the imminent introduction of British Standard Time threatened "to severely curtail or completely halt" their early morning swim.

Margy Sullivan recalls those hardy days: "I think I got hypothermia after my first-ever cold swim," she

RELAXATION I pass young women, serene and subtle from yoga, and teenagers flicking their wet towels flirtatiously at each other after a Lido swim – **Becka Thackray (L55)**

Just being in the open air, relaxing, making lots of friends, it is just so healthy, so much better than indoor pools, it is not a heavy chlorine, it is a much lighter thing. – **Joyce Andrews (L2)**

An oasis of calm and relaxation and a place of well-being – Brockwell Lido was a place you could go and really unwind from the week's labours in the office and simply relax and get in touch with your inner self again. – **Janet Smith (L52)**

says. "I used to run around Brockwell Park and then go for a dip in the Lido, and one day I turned up and there was just some ice and some old people. They had dug a short trench in the ice, so I got in and swam, but the problem was that I didn't have any warm clothes to put on afterwards. I felt pretty awful by the time I got home and couldn't warm up for days. When I did the following year, and with more clothes, I was hooked. Hooked on the feelgood factor."[3.54]

Caroline Russell (L49) joined the Icicles aged 13, around 1960. Like Thelma Phelps in 1937, she was a Mary Datchelor pupil. She says they had a special badge to sew on to their swimming costumes – a sign like a flash of lightning. The rule for joining was that you had to break the ice – or someone did it for you – and then go in the water. They swam all year and she thinks she went in on Christmas Day. She remembers mostly the Sunday mornings, when people would stay an hour or so after their swim. They wore jumpers over their costumes, bare legs and shoes and socks. The men in the group were quite athletic and played a game of hitting a ball against the wall with their hands. She says she didn't remember "any body beautiful stuff".

These were the Icicles who petitioned the Council in 1968 to install floodlights so they could break the ice at their wonted hour. Mindful of the precedent for all Lidos, the GLC wouldn't budge, although the chair of the Arts and Recreation Committee, Harold Sebag-Montefiore, was "concerned that these hardy all-the-year-round open-air swimmers shall not be frustrated". Councillor Hardy (*sic*) asked the chair if Sebag-Montefiore would "establish a precedent of breaking the ice on winter mornings in our open-air swimming pools?" The reply: "Definitely not."[3.55]

That light-hearted interchange above was a rare example of the GLC getting into the detail. When it took over from the LCC in 1965 it had a greater area of London to govern and sought a more strategic role. The micro-management that had characterised 75 years of LCC rule disappeared and in pursuit of that more exalted role the GLC took a step of enormous consequence for the Lido. It decided to devolve all its parks to the charge of the local councils in whose areas they lay.

It sounded simple and an enlightened example of devolving government close to the locality. What it forgot was that a central authority like the LCC or GLC had resources and an economy of scale, neither of which was available to a poor inner-city borough like Lambeth, faced with an increase in its parks area from 33 to 540 acres in one fell swoop.

The strategy was put through with too terrifying speed for Lambeth's liking. On 1971 February 3, with the 1971 April 1 transfer from the GLC of all Lambeth parks only two months away, the LBL Libraries and Amenities Committee sounds in panic: "The available time… is extremely limited and… no detailed official contact had been made by the GLC officers to begin an evaluation of the problems [staff, accommodation, plant, transport and equipment, other factors]… there is an overriding need for an urgent examination of all problems. We are extremely concerned…"[3.56]

A seven-year transitional period cushioned the financial impact of this devolution but its long-term effect was drastic in all areas of Lambeth's sporting and cultural life. The rise to power in 1979 of a Thatcher government bent on curbing the power of the GLC and slapping down poorly-run 'loony left', as she saw it, local authorities like Lambeth (Lambeth councillor 'Red' Ted Knight had parks responsibility at one point) were a deadly cocktail. The Lido, like many other local facilities, suffered in this era and many people interviewed for this book spoke despairingly of the neglect of the pool at this time.

A 1971 LBL Amenity Services Committee report on 'Swimming in Lambeth' bluntly said: "The standard of competitive swimming in Lambeth over the past few years has declined… it was not possible to enter a swimming team in the recent London Youth Games at Crystal Palace, and the Borough Championships are currently of a very low standard"[3.57] – nothing to do with the removal of championships from Brockwell Park Lido in 1969, of course!

In 1971 August, Bernard Perkins, the perhaps partial Conservative ex-Leader of Lambeth Council, drew attention to "litter and filth" at the lido[3.58] – he said "one young mother" went into the Lido café and found "nowhere to sit, but plenty of litter and dirt". The Council meanwhile cut opening hours, increased prices and even tried to charge for the sacred free early-morning winter swim (a quickly reversed decision).[3.59]

To coin another phrase, it was a drip, drip process of attrition. In 1972, diving stages and spring-boards – essential parts of the Lido since 1937 – were removed "because they do not conform with ASA standards". There seems not to have been the imagination or finance to renew, rather than remove them.[3.60] That year, however, saw an attempt by the Council to raise revenue by hiring out rooms in the Lido, with facilities promised for "cards, chess, darts, dominoes, draughts and table-tennis" – though at 50p per weekday session (£1 at weekends), the cashflow may not have been too great to handle.[3.61]

Around this time, the *Times* Diary admitted visiting the Lido: "The fashion show [at the 1977 Earls Court Boat Show] was followed by a display by the Royal Marines which I had already seen during the summer [ie 1976] at Brockwell Park Lido, and then there was some comedy diving which made many people wet."[3.62]

Highlighting the downside of those days isn't always fully representative of how people saw it in the '70s and '80s: Christiane De Montgolfier, born 1923, and a descendant of the brothers who invented the hot air balloon, is a familiar sight, walking her Chihuahua, Candy, in the Park, opposite which she has been living for 30 years. A life-long swimmer who learned to swim in a lake near her village, Charavigne near Grenoble, she loved the Lido: "We all went together and had chats and something to eat, it was nice. Plenty of friends, you make friends quite easily there. You talk to each other. When you start you go by yourself or with one friend, then you meet a lot of other people who are very pleasant and you start talking and so another time you meet again and start talking again and meet more! Then someone would say, 'oh we should swim!' You feel it's good for you. When the days are warm, it's much nicer than when the days are cold, because the water gets quite cold. Still, it's good, all this movement and trying to pass each other, 'oh, I can beat you!'

However, there were two drownings at the Lido in this period. Clinton Marshall, a 14-year-old boy, drowned on 1973 August 16 while lifeguards were distracted having to deal with another swimmer injured by a glass bottle thrown over the Lido wall by "ruffians".[3.63] A decade later, in one of the hottest summers of the 1980s, 18-year-old John Hicks drowned, despite the presence of seven lifeguards,

SEX Girls, girls and more girls (**S155**). Strikingly handsome lifeguards – **Harry Eyres (L23)**

Only one memory surpasses – when, sometime in the late 1960s, I shinned over the wall at midnight with a boyfriend, and, pool to ourselves, we swam by the light of the moon for hours, dried ourselves on his shirt and hopped back over again. Secret, forbidden, luscious… ah, those were great times, before anti-climb paint, absolute-safetyism and ASBO! – **Hylda Sims (L64)**

Sometime in the 1980s, when the asbestos was being removed and there was a temporary changing room poolside, I seduced a lifeguard. He just locked the door when the last man left. Every gay man's fantasy – **Peter Bradley**

Photo: Miranda Payne

on 1983 July 17. There had been a near-drowning a few days previously. 'Death Pool Stays Open,' screamed the front page of July 19's *South London Press*. A week later (July 26), the paper reported Marie Ahern of East Dulwich as saying: "I was horrified at the supervision – or should I say lack of supervision – at the poolside." Parliament Hill Fields, Brockwell's sister Lido, saw the manslaughter of Enrico Sidoli, aged 15 in 1976.[3.64]

Lambeth nurse Hilda Castillo-Binger (L12), born in Tobago, stopped going after hearing of an accident in the Lido where somebody drowned (late 70's/80's) during a hot summer. She came back to

the Lido in the 1990s through fellow health visitor, Jean Castledine, mother of Paddy, one of the duo to take over running the Lido in 1994 (*see Chapter 4*).

Tragedies like these can occur in the best-run of pools – the Coroner at the 1973 inquest said "the safety of this pool is excellent" and blamed the fatality on the act of vandalism – but these two deaths contributed to a general feeling that the Lido was past its best, run-down, not worth supporting.

In 1984, as it headed to its 40th anniversary in 1987, things were not looking good. The Lido was said to be "leaking water at a massive rate", at a cost of £500 a week. Temporary repairs were done to enable it to open for the 1984 summer season but it shut in the autumn for £250,000-worth (about £500,000 today) of repairs, funded by Inner Area Partnership (IAP) money. Typical of the time, the Lido had to shut early at the end of the 1984 season because vandals broke in and spread anti-vandal paint everywhere...[3.65]

The £250,000 IAP money was principally to be used to reline the pool to make it watertight and other planned works included: renewing the poolside, redecorating "throughout", renewing signs, showers, toilets and lighting. The main entrance to the Lido was to be moved to the Dulwich Road side, to enable "the Lido's other facilities to be better used after the Park's closing hours". The gym would be converted into a function room and move to "the vacant café area". Mobile catering vans would enter through an enlarged entrance on the car park side "to enter and operate on the poolside".[3.66]

It sounded, and was, too good to be true. The Lido duly closed for repairs after the summer season of 1984. The pool re-lining went ahead successfully, but work on other areas revealed a disaster: asbestos was found "in quantity, in paneling, and lining the roof". Fixing that alone would cost £300,000, according to local councillor – and Lido supporter – Joan Wailey, "money... that the Council does not have". A temporary fix – spending £30,000 to seal off hazardous areas and provide temporary changing rooms – enabled the summer 1985 season to go ahead, late, on July 14. The front page of the 1985 July *Herne Hill Society Newsletter* was to the point: 'Lido Could Close For Good.' Margaret Hopkins, chair of the Friends of Brockwell Park, suggested starting a 'Support our Lido' campaign, "because if something isn't done, the Lido could close completely and

forever next year".[3.67]

Her analysis was only wrong in its timing. The Lido opened again in 1986 and 1987. In 1988 February, the *Herne Hill Society Newsletter* correctly warned that closure of the Lido was on Lambeth's 'hit-list' for spending cuts: there was no swimming season in summer 1988.[3.67] Protests led to its re-opening again in 1989 and 1990, but it was a wounded institution and Lambeth finally closed it "for good" after the summer 1990 season.[3.68]

Attendance figures for the 1980s tell their tale. Total summer-only swims (comprising Adult, Junior, Free OAP/Disabled and Free Early Morning) for both Kennington and Brockwell Lidos together – separate figures are not given – were (figures in brackets are for Free Early Morning swims – a legacy of the pre-Lido lake period – on which the Council by definition would make no money):

1982 – 25,106 (3370)
1983 – 54,960 (9753)
1984 – 39,379 (9688)
1985 – 17,656 (6598)
1986 – 10,865 (6246)

Another 'what if?' here: if, as the LCC had once attempted, charges had been made for early morning swims, would this have helped the long-term financial prospects of the Lido?

It is a story of highs and lows. The Lambeth Amenity Services Committee is honest enough to say 1986's low attendances "may well reflect the delays in opening... and the uncertainty of the situation which precluded any advance publicity of opening dates" but it also points out a sempiternal truth about Lidos, that "due account should be taken of the relatively unsettled weather in the period".[3.69]

During the period of the Lido's closure (1990–1994), it was squatted and hosted cultural phenomena such as the Exploding Cinema's 'Dive In Show', 1993 July 24. This was a major event showing at least 75 works with an audience of over 2000. Several screenings ran in parallel using the outbuildings and the poolside café as well as projections in the empty pool itself.

Photograph © Patrick Harrison

For over three years, late 1990 to end of 1993, the Lido was in limbo. Lambeth Council had struck a deep blow but withheld a *coup de grâce*. Some took direct action, squatting the quickly derelict building, turning it into a cultural powerhouse with art exhibitions (Andrew Bylo had one in 1992 November, exhibiting paintings that "reveal the strength of community, vitality and resilience of a Lido, whose future is under review") and cinema in the empty pool and surroundings – or, if you prefer, a hippy crashpad and neighbourhood nuisance.

Marty Emery was part of a 'summer of love'-style squat of the Lido: "I was the one who, after five pints of cider, climbed over the wall one evening in April 1993 and changed the locks and had it for a mad summer of events until October.

"I used to work at the Lido as Head Lifeguard and a manager in 1985–6 and knew that the closure was purely political and the Lido was in good condition and the pool worked. I did it to embarrass the Town Hall into finding a way to open it up again and also to have somewhere to live as we used to squat outrageous places back then.

"It was a mad summer of mega film parties/raves that made the *Guardian*'s arts page and the magazines. The Levellers had their after-gig party from the Academy in the shower blocks and Tracey Emin was in a tent there. There was a weekly comedy club and the Brixton Poets held court Fridays and even *Cosmopolitan* held glam photo shoots. The empty pool was a giant cinema and was filled up twice. And all the while the mob of locals and police were at the door, egged on by the *South London Press*."[3.70]

One of the most famous occasions was when local radical film group, the Exploding Cinema, took over the Lido, an event which attracted an audience of over two thousand.[3.71]

Stefan Szczelkun went to the Exploding Cinema event at the Lido: "The 'Dive-In Show' at Brockwell Park Lido was announced in a centre-page advert in an Exploding programme of 1993 July 24. This was a major event showing at least 75 works with a budget of £1200 and a paying audience of over 2000. This was the event that established Exploding Cinema as an underground institution and myth.

"Brockwell Lido at that time was unused and the pool was dry. Changing rooms and other spaces make up about half of the perimeter. These derelict spaces were used to house installations and screenings. This was the Exploding Cinema show that many people remember for the simple reason of its scale. At the time the collective numbered more than 20 people. It provided technical headaches of mammoth proportions. Several screenings ran in parallel using the outbuildings and the poolside cafe as well as projections in the empty pool itself.

"As an audience member, my memory is of experimental, no-budget film culture on an incredible scale. Impressive because of the amount it concentrated into one space, on one evening. Never had I seen so much projection equipment brought into action in one venue.

"On top of that the empty pool did provide a uniquely memorable setting.

"The Lido has a place in the hearts of most people brought up locally. Perhaps the event played some part in the revival of the pool."[3.72]

Caroline Kennedy was part of it: "What I did in the Lido was quite a good installation. It was in the shower room and changing room. I got loads of tiles, and I put that magic stuff which you paint on white tiles and you can print on to it. And I had taken loads of photographs of lidos, people just swimming and lounging. I printed them all on these tiles. And a lot of the tiles were falling off the wall, it was like a really wrecked shower, and I just put them on the ground. And I had a loop of, I think it was me swimming under water, filling the entire space. And there was sound, and smells like bleach. And the sound of water, and people showering, and distant voices."

Douglas Whitton (L60) also went to the Lido in its squatted incarnation: "I remember one night when there was this huge overnight party and film show. It was a documentary of Afghan rebels, which was incredible. It was full screen and most people were sitting in the pool – well not the pool, the pool was empty – watching this documentary film which was surreal but again it was impressive because Marty (Emery) used to pull in maybe 500 people, plus the whole place – in the pool, in the rooms, the whole place – was just full of people."

During the period when the pool was closed and derelict, Roddy Gray (L66) was invited to go back, to run a barbecue there, with his partner. "We took the drums down and did barbecue chicken, jerk chicken, stuff like that." He says he remembers the empty pool, and a guy playing the bagpipes in it. "They were some Urban, Festival group who would take over places that were empty, derelict and make good use of it."

> **SEA** Pleasure of swimming, open environment, flags fluttering in breeze, place to meet people, great asset for our area – like having the sea at the bottom of the road (**S70**). If I can't have the sea I consider it a good second option (**S333**). It's like being beside the seaside without the sand (**S405**). Like being at the seaside but on our doorstep (**S677**). The seaside experience in London – water, sun and relaxed atmosphere and historical remembrance (**S678**)

Casey McGlue (L43) now thinks "the squatters did a good thing – you have to use every bit of the Lido, 365 days a year." The squatters, lively and creative, were not appreciated by all locals, of course. But the Lido – as a swimming venue rather than a squat or a cinema – wasn't short of friends. In 1992 December, Lambeth Councillor Dickson presented a petition of 158 signatures to the Council, urging it to keep the Lido open. According to Robert Holden of the FOBP, this spurred Lambeth's Environmental Services Committee into action. In 1993, the Council placed notices in newspapers "seeking proposals from commercial operators and voluntary and other groups to operate the Lido complex, with an obligation to run a public swimming service for at least eight weeks between July and September. There would be no subsidy or funding from the Council, and no fee would be charged by the Council."[3.73]

This was a gift horse into whose mouth several looked but whose reins few sought to grasp. By the end of 1993, nothing had come of this initiative by the Council. All signs were that the Council felt it had exhausted all options and would move to the *coup de grâce* and kill the Lido for good. A mild-mannered, diffident article entitled 'Eau or Dough?' appeared in the October 1993 (no. 15) *Newsletter* of the Friends of Brockwell Park. Its author was the mild-mannered, diffident Michael Boyle. "We call on the Council to make a commitment to one of Lambeth's most prized and valued assets," he gently said.

The Friends of Brockwell Park and other local campaigners had been involved in several campaigns for the Park – fighting against a running track, for the 1 O'Clock Club and restoring the café in Brockwell Hall after the fire. People like Sheila Northover, Robert Holden and Michael Boyle mounted one of the most effective campaigns the Lido has ever had. In a whirlwind five weeks, a Friends of Brockwell Park 'Save the Lido' team collected almost 5000 signatures – 4674 to be precise, as Michael likes to be; up to that time, the largest petition ever presented to Lambeth Council. It simply said: "We, the undersigned, call on Lambeth Council to re-open the Brockwell Park Lido and take whatever action is necessary to secure its long-term future."

Boyle (L5) had moved to Herne Hill around 1980 specifically to be close to the Lido, which he describes as "very neglected" at that time. He found himself swimming with about two other people – and got used to "having this Lido completely to myself". Although he was an unlikely water warrior, he became active on the committee, which "got helpers wherever they could, who took areas, went round knocking on doors asking for signatures". His parkside flat was "a central point to meet, have a drink and go out collecting and come back with signatures. People went up and down their road in their own time." There were different 'Save Our Lido' posters – and petition forms in lots of shops.

Linda Spashett (L53) was a member of the Friends of Brockwell Park but had not done anything very active until the Friends started a petition in 1993 to get the pool reopened. She got signature sheets and helped collect signatures at the fireworks on 1993 November 5, in the Park at the weekends and joined the Friends when they knocked on doors on a dark November evening to collect signatures. She remembers getting 50 signatures on one day in the Park.

Michael Boyle presented the petition to Lambeth's Environmental Services Committee on

The flip side of Lido life (1957): swimming in the rain…
Photographer unknown. Reproduced by kind permission of London Metropolitan Archives.

1993 December 3, given three minutes to make the case: "It was fairly nerve-wracking – I was desperately trying to get over the importance of the Lido, apart from swimming, from a social, local point of view...

"One councillor said, 'We already have swimming available at Brixton Rec. What's different about what the Lido offers?' I remember, it was so obvious what was different, but I was struggling to articulate it in the short time I had. The name that got given to it later, 'Brixton Beach' – that's all I need have said. This is where grandmothers come with their children and have a picnic – does that happen in Brixton Rec? All day?"

It worked. Committee chair Councillor Janet Crook thanked the FOBP for the petition and the Committee decided to explore in depth one of the consortium proposals for privately running the Lido. The following year, that consortium, led by two young entrepreneurs, Paddy Castledine and Casey McGlue, re-opened Brockwell Park Lido…

July 1956 championships: overcast skies and pouring rain marred the two Area Meetings on July 14 for the few spectators who attended.

Timeline 3: 1935–1993, from Opening to Closing

1935 LCC announces three-year Lido-building programme 1937 July 10 – Brockwell Lido opens July 13 – LCC promises to make London 'a City of Lidos' 1938 LCC takes over maintenance of all Lidos from local authorities 1939 Ahead of war, Lido made capable of providing water for Fire Brigade / Free swimming classes at Lido 1939–1945: War Lido opened every year for summer season and partly for winter season / Galas held 1942, '43, '45 ('44 Gala cancelled because of flying bomb attacks) 1946 Lido opens for summer season 1947–1968 Swimming Championship Area meetings every year for 22 years at Lido, which also hosted Finals on nine occasions 1952 £9319 spent on repairing war damage at Lido 1958 Separate arrangements for spectators abolished 1960 £1833 spent re-laying Lido paving / Wolfenden Report on Sport and the Community comes down on side of indoor pools 1961 Lockers replace baskets for clothes storage 1965 GLC takes over from LCC 1968 Brockwell Icicles unsuccessfully lobby GLC for floodlighting for winter morning swims 1971 GLC transfers parks to local authorities – Brockwell Park and Lido become responsibility of London Borough of Lambeth 1972 Diving stages and spring-boards removed 1973 Clinton Marshall, 14, drowns at the Lido 1983 John Hicks, 18, drowns at the Lido 1984 Lido shuts for £250,000-worth of repairs; asbestos discovered 1988 No summer swimming season 1990–1993 Pool, closed by Lambeth Council, gets squatted; used for art displays/performance/cinema 1992 Petition of 158 signatures, asking LBL to keep pool open 1993 Michael Boyle leads campaign to save Lido – over 4000 signatures collected / Lambeth Council decides to see if it can outsource Lido 1994 LBL offers seven-year lease to young entrepreneurs, Paddy Castledine and Casey McGlue

Loving the Lido – Hylda Sims (2004)

We're doing our best to save it
from people who say development
unviable and forward-planning
too often,
who find it possible
to stand quite near the edge
with their clipboards and gray suits
their feet covered in shoes, their skin
never touching the water
of our Lido

We're doing our best to save it
from dull councillors and smart business persons
consortiums and quangos
hot indoor baths, jacousies and saunas
fitness centres with buttock-reducing contraptions
and television screens
(in case you get bored on the running machines)
where, ipod in place, you try
to work out what those moving pictures mean.

> Here, the water gives and takes light
> wind ripples it
> swimmers rearrange it in arcs and arrowheads
> their heads dipping and turning, their hands
> scattering diamonds back, oh
> the glide and splash, the dive and flash of them
> in our lido sixty-seven years beautiful. Ivies
> have scaled its LCC brick walls, trees
> grown old and tall outside, inside: a mirage
> a trompe l'oeil, an urban miracle
> this oblong isle
> this shining pool, always
> warmer, bluer than the sky, set
> in its emerald sea, reminding us
> who we are, how we were

We're doing our best to save it
from cost-benefit analysts
public-private partnerships, regulators
inspectors and architects, their hard hats
on hard heads
supervising wrecking balls, bulldozers,
diggers and cranes, progressing
their multi-level shopping mall and car park, plus
underground plunge facility
but who have made no plans for
the pair of mallard ducks
flying over from the park every evening
to join other late swimmers
in our lido

We're doing our best to save it
for the heavily pregnant young woman
now breast-stroking up and down the centre of the pool, while
her soon-to-be-born son sails under the water
in his womb-boat
backbone to the deep
dreaming now, not kicking his heels, oh
the rock and flow of it, the to and fro of it, so
this is what it's going to be like
he feels…

We're doing our best to save it
for you, little one
but so few of us are left

(from *Sayling the Babel*, poems and songs by Hylda Sims published by
Hearing Eye 2006) www.hylda.co.uk, www.hearingeye.org

In the deep end: Paddy Castledine (left) and Casey McGlue sample the dry facilities.

Chapter 4

From 1994 Re-opening to 2007

'The Lido is a special place you know, it is not only me know that, everybody knows that. Lambeth knows that, the government knows that. It is different from all Lidos.'
– Sammy Dangerous

'Does each era get the Lido it deserves? Discuss…'

An interesting exam question, looking down the decades, but especially for the 'Paddy and Casey' era of 1994–2002. At nine years this was one of the briefest in the Lido's history yet one which for many has already assumed the character of a golden age.

Paddy Castledine (L13) and Casey McGlue (L43) were an unlikely pair: Paddy "the posh one" – he says 'Leedo' – and Casey "the rough diamond" – he says 'Lie-do'. Paddy describes the relationship with Casey as "interesting – we had huge respect for each other. It wasn't always easy, but we never came to blows! We complemented each other. We grew up together at the Lido. It was a huge responsibility for two lads to take on. But the best thing – it worked. Now we're both busy building up new careers and families so we don't see each other much. We had good times, we lived out of each other's pockets for over a decade, like husband and wife, I'm not saying who's which…"

For Casey, "Paddy and I are very different characters. I'm more socialist and he's more conservative. But in the first year we were thrown in at the deep end and just got on with it. We were so busy, trying to do too much ourselves, trying to build up the winter side of things. Paddy and I were never close friends, we were just people who knew

each other through sport. We had our stand-up rows, of course, but we just got on with it and helped it work. I'm a bit of a hippy, I like to party, Paddy is a little bit straighter and squarer. It was easier to work together rather than get rid of each other! Sometimes opposites work."

It all started on a wing and a prayer. Faced in 1993 with the biggest petition ever presented to it, Lambeth Council felt it had to do something about the Lido. Unsurprisingly, there had been few takers when it had advertised for "proposals from commercial operators and voluntary and other groups" to operate the Lido complex. The offer was that there was to be an obligation to run a public swimming service for at least eight weeks every summer, with no subsidy or funding from the Council, even if no fee would be charged by the Council.

Under pressure from the Friends of Brockwell Park petition at the end of 1993 (*see Chapter 3*), Lambeth Council looked again at the proposals that had come in and decided to offer Brockwell Park Lido to two ex-employees (ex- because Lambeth had made them redundant in a previous cost-cutting round): Paddy Castledine (L13) and Casey McGlue (L43). McGlue had been a Lambeth Sports Officer and had taught canoeing and fitness at the

Lido, and had met Castledine who had done stints there as duty manager.

Paddy Castledine's (L13) first memories are of a summer holiday at the Lido, where he and his twin brother learned to swim in the late 60s, taught by his Mum, Jean (L14). She would pack a picnic, they would bag a bench and then "We'd walk in at the shallow end holding hands, then do 'ring a ring a rosies, all fall down' and that's how we got in."

In 1984, the summer of his first year at university (Kent, studying Physical Education), and at his mum's prompting, he applied for a job as a lifeguard at the Lido, something he did for the summers till it closed in 1990.

It was a revelation: "At the age of 19, to be the keyholder of this fantastic venue... I made the most of it, always on early shift. And in the years I was running the Lido, only once it didn't open at 6.45, when I overslept. The key element was reliability, it's more than just a job, even if you had a hangover or buses weren't working, you had a responsibility to so many people for their happiness: it was the start of their day, they didn't want their life ruined!"

It was at the Lido that Paddy first met Casey, who coached schoolkids in canoeing from 10-12, the fallow period between end of morning swims and start of the main public swim session: "Casey would rock up with a bunch of canoes and kids. We hit it off, we both loved rugby. I played fly half, Casey captained Harlequins."

In 1993, a friend of McGlue's phoned and said, "Have you heard the Lido is up for tender?" McGlue was playing rugby for Paddy's old boys' team, the Old Blues and they both – with their working knowledge of the Lido – decided to give it a go. Castledine said: "We both thought, we've nothing to lose. We got in touch with a Council officer – and I think the Council saw the same, nothing to lose and everything to gain. They probably thought it wouldn't work; they underestimated the drive and persistence and good fortune we enjoyed."

A news presenter for Channel 4 helped write the business proposal "and to my amazement we got it", said McGlue. Their vision was "to use the spaces all year round, because you can't survive on the summer stuff". They were young, both in their 20s, they were bold – and they didn't really know what they were letting themselves in for: "You'll probably laugh – we had no idea what we were doing," McGlue said. "We had to talk about staff, equal opportunities, security, charges. We told them we had money; we didn't have any money."

They did have lots of friends and local people who helped with repairs, painting, fixing it up. There was a wonderful photo in the *Independent* of the vast empty pool getting the finishing touches.[4.1]

They got given the keys to the Lido in 1994 February and soon there were yoga and kids classes up and running (*see box on Stakeholders*). After a three-year gap, the Lido was opened for its 1994 summer season by 'Brockwell Lido Ltd'. They had beginners' luck – 1994 and 1995 were gloriously hot and the Lido was jumping. Up to 2004, morning swim sessions ended at 10am and as often as not there would be a bucket inside the Dulwich Road entrance for your (reduced) admission charge. The pool re-opened at midday, with access via the main entrance on the south, park-facing side – and that's when the crowds came, on the sunny days.

Their Year 1 focus, says Castledine, was "to get the pool open so people could get back swimming, get a sense of what the place is all about. Why were these places built in the first place? For people, for families to have a day out which felt like a

FAMILY-FRIENDLY I always bring a packed lunch. It is a day out. As a single parent it is a nice place to come with my children and we meet lots of new people (S260)

It is child-friendly and safe, a unique resource within the area (S306)

Not many places like this left, a good family day out. A part of history (S385)

There's not much in Lambeth for the whole family to attend (S585)

My children and I have a good time every time we come here and it is a cheap day out for us on low income (S591)

week, to give them a holiday because they couldn't afford one, an escape from pressures. Between those four walls you could be anywhere, it was up to your imagination."

A trip to the cash-and-carry market bought £100-worth of fizzy drinks and crisps; they sold the lot and doubled their money and soon had to take on staff to sell the stuff: "it was all trial and error."

From the beginning, the unique elements of the Paddy & Casey style were established. They were young and relaxed, they *were not* the Council, not bureaucratic.

Their attitude transmitted itself to the lifeguard staff, young and laidback. Quirky announcements in the rich West Indian tones of 'Dangerous' became treasured for their irascible abruptness – "Stop blocking the car park *now*!" or the incantatory "Please put your rubbish in the bins, not the floor. Please put your rubbish in the bins, not the floor. If you don't mind you can take it home with you, but please do not leave it on the floor."

For early morning swimmers, the wooden refreshment hut in the south-east corner became an institution – good coffee and generous slices of toast slowly made by a sexy South African lifeguard in what looked like an authentic Art Deco machine. A wobbly black plastic table held tubs of marge and jars of Marmite and marmalade bristling with white plastic knives.

Great parties and barbecues were held, fireworks set off on the roof. People held their weddings or their birthdays (Peter Bradley held his 50th there in 2000) at the Lido. Dom Holmes (L33) and Jane Austin (L4) got married at the Lido in 2001: "It was local and it was outdoor, there was the pool and we got flares and… there was a wonderful atmosphere." They had a fancy dress

theme and a Frank Sinatra tribute band. "Really memorable, with kids swimming about at night, the Frank Sinatra band, everyone dressed up and drinking cocktails…" Zoe Burt and her husband Rupert got wed at the Lido in 2003 September. Rupert pulled Zoe in the boat across the pool. Additional drama and energy was provided by small children swimming alongside and hauling themselves into the boat. And, of course, Paddy had his own wedding there, in 2000. At the Lido he met a major sports agent: "We used to read the *Racing Post* together, won a load of money and bought a racehorse, which we called Brockwell Lido. One day he said, 'you must meet my bank manager, Sasha' and I did and we fell in love and I married her at the Lido – it was one of my dreams to get married there." They had 200 guests, and Paddy boated his wife across the pool, and Paddy the ex-choral scholar sang 'Where E'er You Walk' from *Semele* by Handel to her.

Each season, Paddy and Casey tried to add something new – plants by the pool, a mural on the principal façade (naughty!) or Japanese-style flags flapping along the roof. I remember early summer mornings when I would gaze out of my tower block overlooking the Lido and see Paddy dive in on his own into a Lido empty but for a few ducks. Heaven was it then to be alive…

The lifeguards were key to the success of those summers. "The way we were with our staff reflected through to the customers," said McGlue. "We didn't have a million rules and that attracted good staff, which is difficult because it's seasonal work. But we retained core staff who then trained up the green people each year."

Paddy said there was no recruitment drive for lifeguards. Their sporting contacts and word of

The Yoga Room at the Lido's deep end. Yoga teacher Nigel Gilderson is directly in front of the door that gives on to the pool.

Photo: Miranda Payne

mouth brought people to the Lido door; and everyone was given a week's trial – typical of their trusting approach to human relations. Crucial, though, was Nigel 'Dog' Bowlden – "a freshfaced South African, champion lifeguard, head lifeguard material, great communicator with users, public and staff and me and Casey. He's living in Wales, still phones on a hot day and says, 'what would we be doing down the Lido on a day like this?'"

Senior lifeguard Howard Cunnell recalls the pattern of the job: "The season started off very quietly and built up and up. In late May you got the regulars who couldn't wait for it to open, and swam

and didn't moan about how cold the water was. Once schools broke up, the whole character of the place changed.

"Mornings became best time, to be quite honest, regular people having breakfast and mellow; about 11 or 12 it would start building up and building up till capacity 1500. Really busy day, intensity building up with crowds, not just about watching water, also had to negotiate various tensions and difficulties that arise when you have a large number of people sitting close to each other in the heat, different tribes, tensions heat. Crowds queuing up before it opens. Long queues waiting

Three Lido Stakeholders:
Yoga, Whippersnappers, Buddhists

YOGA: Nigel Gilderson (L26) remembers "just putting some flyers through some doors… and on the first day I had over 19 people coming into a tiny little space without knowing me or knowing what yoga is about. So there has always been a demand in this area and an interest in yoga."

Gilderson's first impression was definitive: "I just remember seeing that expanse and thinking, yes, we've arrived."

Co-manager Casey McGlue said: "We weren't big corporate, we didn't have a million rules." This definitely extended to the financial arrangements, Gilderson says: 30% of the takings to the Lido, whatever they were, "so that if we had one or two students we were not out of pocket for the rent; an ideal way to set something up without going through the normal channels of setting up businesses and rental agreements and tenancies; there was never any real commercial pressure to make it anything other than what it is and I feel really privileged to have been able to go through that experience. It is literally just trusting the process of whatever it is you are teaching, whether yoga or anything. Just having a forum for that process to take place in is enough to generate its own life."

Gilderson came to the Lido because he was friends with Casey and attributes much of its magic to his personality: "It was the marriage between the particular nature of the place and Casey's nature that made it, for a while, exceptional."

Gilderson has blazed a trail for yoga at the Lido. Fellow yoga teacher Julia Williams (L61) says: "It's quite special as a place. Go down to teach a class and the ducks have hatched their little ducklings in the corner of the pool. We had that nice long room at the top of the pool – hundreds of people outside and just doing something calm and peaceful inside." Colleague Paul Duffy (L21) remembers challenging times: "Teaching yoga and youth climbing over the roof and kicking the door down – security was non-existent."

WHIPPERSNAPPERS: Caroline Burghard, like Gilderson and McGlue ("I'm a bit of a hippy") came from an alternative background, studying mime in Paris after dropping out of school. By 1993, with a daughter to care for, she had "a deeper feeling about what life was about" and was doing voluntary work at Effra School toddler group, "singing with the kids". Then, in 1994, "*Brixton Village* magazine came through my door with this tiny little ad: 'Brockwell Lido looking for people to run workshops'."

She turned up at the Lido, without appointment, rang the doorbell and Casey and Paddy came to the door, "two young, charming bachelors". They showed her up to the yoga rooms "and it was idyllic because Nigel [Gilderson] had already moved in there, yellow walls, red carpet and it had that yoga vibe, perfect". She phoned around and got 15 people to turn up to the first class, and experienced the less wonderful side of lack of bureaucracy: "I turned up, Paddy said, 'oh, sorry, double-booked you but we've got this room down here, the function room'. A massive space with blue lino, really like a squat, no atmosphere, but I had to do it because I had 15 people turning up. It went really well. The next week 20 people turned up, then the next week 30, then I had to put on two classes."

There was more of the same: "There were times when I'd come in to the function room and I'd find a pair of knickers on the floor from the night before, whether it was people climbing over the wall or lifeguards, it was a bit like that." Her memory of that early period is "it was buzzing. Those first three years were just amazing".

By 1997, Burghard, with her business partner Kirk Service, was running a major community company. It organised a 2000-strong event in the dry Lido to launch a tape they'd made, of a new kind of music called 'Pickney Beat' and was looking for a name after its first choice, Teenyboppers, turned out to be already licensed: "We stayed up all night looking in every book and came up with the name 'Whippersnappers'. Now we do all ages, but we've all got the child within us and it's quite an intriguing name."

Although Whippersnappers is now London-wide, the Lido seems a sort of spiritual home for Burghard: "I have been in this building more than anyone else in the last 13 years, spend nearly 70 hours a week here. I love the spirit of it, it's got a really strong sense, people come through the door and feel they're at home." The strong characters who have populated the Lido since 1994 are what have made it for her: "There was a beautiful lifeguard called Oona here in the first three years and we set up a kids club, arts and craft, treasure hunt and she was part of it. Very sadly she got run over and died – and she's still in this building for me." Casey McGlue also mentioned Oona in moving terms.

BUDDHISTS: A little-known feature of the Lido is that, since 2000, there has been Buddhist meditation there, at first just on Monday evenings and now on Thursday evenings too. Satyanathin, who leads the sessions, has been a member of the FWBO (Friends of the Western Buddhist Order) since 1984, and has been teaching for more than 12 years, largely in South London. When the Clapham community folded the FWBO group moved to the Lido, at the suggestion of lifeguard Catherine, an FWBO member. Satyanathin sees yoga as complementary to meditation: "In fact meditation is a form of yoga, making the mind more flexible. People enjoy meditating, because people are committed to it and enjoy being in concentrated states and deepening their sense of connection with their depth of being. We are able to offer people ideals, without the Lido we couldn't have done it, so it's saved something really valuable."

For former Fusion Lido manager Rob Pagano (L46), the biggest challenge of his job was getting to know all the different stakeholders involved "and being able to provide something that makes it workable for all those different stakeholders. Being able to bring them all in under one umbrella and deliver a product and service that all of them like and can take ownership of… still today that's the biggest challenge."

Oo aarr, me hearties: Whippersnapper pirates take over the Lido.

Photo: courtesy of Whippersnappers

for two hours outside. 1500 people come in and then we lock the gates for two hours and bring the shutters down. Meanwhile outside, people's tempers fray, people taking car-jacks to the steel shutters, try and get in or climb over wall. Days you remember are the days when you are tested as a lifeguard and you come through it. In all the years I worked there we never had a fatal accident, not once. I am very proud of this, not just for me but from everyone's point of view."

In a novel in progress, Cunnell gives a good idea of what it *felt like* to be a lifeguard:

"What can I tell you? Things are different now. Up here and for as long as this English summer lasts I feel entire, myself undivided. I am very tan. All of the Lifeguards are tan. We sit in high blue chairs under the sun in this August early morning, dark sentinels above the water. My bare caramel feet, tattooed with blue Hibiscus flowers, rest crossed on the diving board that comes out from under my chair like a jetty incomplete. I can taste sun oil, coffee, and skunkweed in the air. I shouldn't smoke the skunk, not at this time of day for sure and probably not at all anymore, but I'd love a short black coffee right now. High above me police helicopters circle over Brixton in the warming air."

Channel swimmer and Lido lifeguard Victor Malwa eyes his Brixton Channel.

Photo: Miranda Payne

Victor Malwa (L42), born 1979, has been a lifeguard at the Lido since 2001. He was the first Sub-Saharan African to swim the English Channel, in August 2005. He says: "40% of my Channel training was at the Lido, I used to swim lengths to practise there in the morning and the evening, so the Lido is my other Channel."

When Victor got back to the Lido after his successful swim, Dangerous announced it to everyone: "It was amazing to see, even people who seemed not to be interested in swimming."

Crispin Levy (L39) is a 'typical' example of a career trajectory in the post-1994 Lido. At 13, he took over some bucket-minding shifts in the early mornings, progressing to general dogsbody. He remembers helping to insert someone's nose ring in its piercing because there was no mirror in the men's changing room. Eventually, in 2000, Crispin was taken on as a lifeguard. He had had the RLSS qualification but Paddy and Casey were strict about employing only mature lifeguards. He spent several summers in the lifeguard team, alternately topping up his tan or huddling under an umbrella. The high point of his association with the Lido so far was in 2006 February, with his production of David Hare's *The Blue Room* in the cafe-transformed into a-theatre. The three-night run was a sell-out, possibly because of a warning on the posters about scenes of semi-nudity!

A different take on Paddy and Casey comes from Cypriot Tai Chi teacher, Andreas Demetriou (L18). He first discovered the Lido in 1976. He remembers a gym in what was later the yoga room: "One morning the equipment had disappeared." For Andreas, Tai Chi "represents the same spirit of easy-going and quiet approach to everything that the Lido people had – the new age approach". He had an unusual solution to the problem of the Icicle effect of the early morning swim: "I decided that heat and cold are just sensations and you get used to it."

As well as setting the ambience, Castledine and McGlue also went about their vision of all-round use of the space. Two key people came along in the opening year: Nigel Gilderson (L26), yoga teacher and Caroline Burghard (L6), running classes for children (*see Stakeholders box*).

The London Borough of Lambeth gave the Lido a grant of £30,000–£40,000 a year for the first four years – "a drop in the ocean", says McGlue, in an apt turn of phrase. They had got a seven-year lease at a peppercorn rent from Lambeth because the Lido was derelict and a 100% discount on business rates because they were rejuvenating it and giving employment: "We were doing all that without knowing we were doing it. Lambeth had all the political rhetoric, we were actually doing it," says McGlue.

When that grant stopped, along with the good weather, the precarious nature of Lido finances – a theme throughout its history – came sharply to the fore. The pressure on the pair to make money became intense. They held more parties, they sold alcohol – a strange thing for a sports facility and something of which McGlue says "I wasn't proud... but it helped pay the bills".

They became ever more resourceful: they did parties, Tai Chi, film shoots, adverts, location shots. Perhaps the most famous film made about the Lido was Lucy Blakstad's 1995 documentary in the BBC Modern Times series, called simply *The Lido*. The stunning imagery was matched by equally startling words: "Outside, I'm surrounded by labels – gay, white, HIV man. Here, I'm just Craig." Or: "I couldn't afford a holiday this year – and here is like a hotel anywhere in the world." Or the man from Northern Ireland whose solution for its troubles was original: "Get a Lido in Belfast and sling them all in it and let them get on with each other!" A famous moment was when Robin Butler (L8) – now Lord Butler of Brockwell and then Margaret Thatcher's Cabinet Secretary, "chief engineer in the engine room of government" – was captured in a state of undress, due to the Brixton mistral blowing his towel at a crucial moment. "The next morning, when I arrived for work at Downing Street, the policeman on duty said, 'No need to show your pass, Sir – I recognise you even with your clothes on' and a member of my office said, 'I saw that you had a small part in that television programme last night'!" Andrew Turnbull (now Lord Turnbull), Principal Private Secretary to Thatcher, often joined him – and so the Prime Minister's Cabinet Secretary and PPS both started their days in Brockwell Park Lido. The lesbian partnership ceremony at the end gives a flavour both of the film and of that era of the Lido.

Paddy and Casey even persuaded Evian to take up a major £100,000 sponsorship. 'Evian' was painted on the bottom of the pool, which was renamed the Evian Lido for a while. Finlay, a

Photo: Al de Perez

2am. The police would know they were there in the building but didn't do anything because they knew that everyone was enjoying themselves. They carried on meeting there for over five years... "It was a place we went... to play dominoes... for fun!" And he used to swim there all the time: "I love the Park; I love all the trees."

The late night parties caused local resentment. Michael Boyle (L5), one of the stalwarts of the 1993 campaign to save the Lido, whose flat is all too close to it, said: "It became an absolute menace... They were taken to court and fined for a breach of the… whatever. It marred things, an unfortunate time. The origin was that there was not a proper financial basis. They were living hand-to-mouth doing whatever they could." The Friends of Brockwell Park wrote to the council, says Boyle, telling it in effect: "You can't just sling your problem into somebody else's lap and expect them to solve it. Subsidy must go on."

Castledine says: "I would do it all again if I could. You don't miss something till you're out of there. I really mourn the Lido. There's a part of me that's a little bit aggrieved with what the Council is doing. You'd think they could see what we've done and give us a longer lease to make it work, but that's not how councils work. And we made enemies, we made mistakes, we had to survive, we loved functions, and it did get noisy, the Lido is a huge amphitheatre." That wistful note is there: "I still mourn it greatly – when you're there you don't realise how great a thing you have. It's almost as if the Lido is human, it rewards you: if you look after it, it will look after you."

In 1996, LIFT – London International Festival of Theatre – did a five-month project in Brockwell Park with Christophe Berthonneau, says Rose de Wend

neighbour of mine in the tower block, said he used to look at the huge 'Evian' sign and dream he saw a 'D' before it and a 'T' after. Evian pulled out of the sponsorship a year later: Brockwell Lido wasn't "national enough" says McGlue.

George Walters (L66) remembers meeting with his Dominoes Club at the Lido when the pool was empty. As many as 50 people attended, including his wife and Olive Morris who played with the group: "Even Casey joined the Club at one stage!" It was free to play and was run on a volunteer basis, and they used to raise their own funds, and would raise money for local causes. Sometimes the sessions would go on "All Night!" – or at least until

Fenton (L20), LIFT co-director for 25 years. Berthonneau, the world's top pyrotechnician, "a flaming French wizard", worked with 120 teenagers from Stockwell Park School, culminating in a wonderful performance in the Park. The Lido played its small part in the event, hosting the thank-you party for kids and sponsors, Fenton says: "It was June, a beautiful sunny evening with a chilly wind. It was just a fantastic gathering at the Lido with the water shimmering, hearing all the preparations in the park, seeing all the children gathering, hearing the music being tested out."

McGlue reckons "you need £250,000 a year minimum to run a Lido – that's what the Corporation of London under-writes Parliament Hill Fields Lido for. We were trying to run Brockwell Park Lido for nothing. Things had to change; we were running on the spot just to survive."

The one sure thing was that the Council would *not* subsidise the Lido and with McGlue and Castledine only having a seven-year lease, there was little incentive for them to seek long-term investment in the Lido. By 2001, there was universal agreement with McGlue's analysis that "things had to change", but no resolution in sight. Lambeth gave the pair a one-year extension to their lease (to 2002), promising to use the summer of 2001 to consult locally on the best way forward.

The steer came from an unlikely source: three feisty local women. Judy Holman (L30), Mary Hill (L32) and Yvonne Levy (L40) knew each other from their residents' association but each found their way separately to the Lido for early-morning swims – and started having beach-hut breakfasts together, as you do… It was 2001 August, the end of season was looming, and there was not a whiff of a Lambeth Council consultant, when market

Photo: Al de Perez

researcher Yvonne Levy, mindful of the work the Friends of Brockwell Park had done in the past, said to her companions the immortal line: "The Lido needs some 'Friends'."

The three, with Paddy and Casey's blessing, called a meeting for Sunday 2001 August 12, 7pm in the café, cunningly offering a free swim from 6pm to boost attendance. "It was very instinctive," said Judy Holman. A plain A4 flyer was handed out, headed 'Friends of the Lido', followed by: "We love the Lido. If you love the Lido too please read on!!" (only two exclamation marks would do). Paddy and Casey were to give an update on the Lido and it was very firmly stated that "a Steering Group will be set up to take things forward". Mary Hill says: "From that meeting of 70 or more we drew a committee of 12/13 and it was excellent."

By the next (multi-coloured, but mostly blue) flyer, announcing a meeting for 'Thurday' 2001 September 13, the group had a name: Blu – Brockwell Lido Users. The flyer stated its vision of the place loud and clear: "Brockwell Lido… is one of the few community resources that has never dated and still represents a sanctuary right in the heart of the city. It still has a magic that no indoor or covered pool could ever offer." The flyer went on to describe 'Blu' as "a group of people who feel passionately that Brockwell Lido is a vital community resource", whose aim was "to offer a voice for all those people in the community who want the Lido to stay open, as an open-air pool".

In the absence of any Council initiative, the group made a key decision – to get swimmers' – and other users such as yoga students' – views of what sort of Lido they wanted before the Lido shut after the summer season. Yvonne Levy's skills as a market researcher came into their own, from design – "I wanted a lot of open-ended questions, the only way to capture what people loved about the Lido" – to collecting and analysis. There was a staggering response, with 874 surveys returned: "We had 100% response rate, which is impossible, you don't get it. No refusals at all," said Levy. "No-one could read those 874 questionnaire responses without being moved, impressed, chastened – chastened at the thought that such a communal poetic articulation of how a treasured amenity is so seldom elicited and so often overruled by bureaucratic considerations," said Harry Eyres (L23).

The meticulously analysed Survey was a powerful entrée to the Council. It showed the wide range of users and their many hopes for the Lido, dispelling some Councillors' belief that it was just a white, middle-class enclave. Lambeth appointed leisure consultants Torkildsen Barclay to come up with options for the Lido's future and Ian Barclay – having had the benefit of 847 surveys, among other inputs – duly presented his report in 2001 November.

Around this time, but before the Barclay report had been published, Mary Hill and Yvonne Levy, by now representing Brockwell Lido Users, met Lambeth Labour Councillor Paul McGlone, executive member for the environment. He was sympathetic, saying he wanted to get the right rather than the easy solution. He agreed on the importance of the Lido's community dimension but stressed the importance of finding a way to generate sufficient money to make the investment the Lido needed. He felt Lambeth Council might work with BLU (no longer 'Blu'), provided it was properly constituted.[42] His other query was: Is BLU 'neutral'? "He really wanted to know if we were coming in with one solution," said Mary Hill, as opposed to going where the evidence led. Not neutral about saving the Lido, BLU told McGlone it would seek to be pragmatic and flexible about *how* it might be saved. "The wonderful thing about BLU from the very beginning," says Mary Hill, "was that no one came in with a private agenda. The agenda was always, we want to save the Lido, but on the whole we were willing to look at the options." She says that although there was a very strong attachment to Paddy and Casey, BLU members "were also rational enough to know we had to look at what was realistic".

But there were Councillors on both sides of the political divide keen to make progress. When the

Model of the 2006–2007 Lido project. Extending the southern pavilion of the Lido five metres into the Park gives about an extra 1500sq mtrs. This will contain year-round gym/spa facilities, which will subsidise the Lido when summers are less summery...

Plan courtesy PTEA Architects

Conservatives took power, another powerful person took up cudgels. Conservative Lambeth Councillor Clare Whelan (L59) was Executive Member for the Environment in 2002, steering the Lido project through at a time when all the advice said there was no way that an open-air Lido could pay its way: "Thank goodness Paddy and Casey took on that challenge with, I think, the goodwill of most of the local community behind them but with the concern of some within the Council who liked to do things in an orderly way and have a structure to things," Councillor Whelan said. The Lido did have a very special atmosphere, she added: "It did not feel like a functional Council facility. It was very embedded into the community and there was a strong commitment to preserving it." She believes "quite an imaginative solution was arrived at – to get a not-for-profit organisation running it and try to get a community steering group". She says everyone realised that without making the Lido bigger it could not survive and couldn't provide the rooms and facilities that it needed: "Let us hope that what we have done is robust enough to withstand time, that the investment that has been put in will build a stronger fabric, will actually last. I just hope that generations of children grow up loving it and committed to it being there."

The BLU Steering Group was given the Barclay

ARCHITECTURE
It has a lovely spaciousness, the proportions are right. – **Andreas Demetriou (L18)**

It's like a little magic kingdom, you know, you've got these wonderful 1930s walls, like a little gated city, like a haven of tranquillity. It's just always meant so much to me. – **Helen Fensterheim (L24)**

Amazing to be in a city surrounded by noise and traffic and you walk through a door and it just all disappears and you have this high energy laughter and I like the idea of the Lido being Brixton Beach because I think it is amazing the difference between the inside of the door and the outside of the door – **Cindy Afflict (L1)**

The Lido from Park View House, a tower block overlooking the Lido. All during the 2006-2007 refurbishment, the red boat lay beached in the dry pool.

Photo: Jo Edwards, PTEA

report at the end of 2001 December and was able to circulate its gist to the membership, ahead of an open meeting Lambeth had called in 2002 January to discuss it. So BLU was perhaps the best prepared of all the interest groups represented at the meeting and cunningly made sure its members spread themselves round all the breakout groups. When it came to selecting a Steering Group representing all Lido stakeholders, facilitators agreed that three out of its six members should be delegates from BLU.

This Lido Steering Group – not the same as the BLU Steering Group, of course – has been in the driving seat of community involvement ever since

and is part of the future structure of the Lido. Mary Hill describes it as "an amazing group" that "worked as a team despite heated discussions". It quickly drew up six criteria for any long-term settlement:

1 Retain an open-air swimming pool with at least the present opening hours and seasons.
2 Retain and expand existing community use, with health and learning activities like yoga, Tai Chi, Whippersnappers, meditation.
3 Keep the Lido in keeping with the park and the local neighbourhood.
4 Have community representation in the future management.

MY REASON TO BE IN LAMBETH Open early in morning, a great way to start the day. The Lido is the most important facility in Lambeth for me (S64)

The Lido is uniquely important as part of the fabric of Herne Hill. It should be preserved at all costs. (S74)

It is like having an instant holiday on your doorstep – I have just moved house so I could be close to the Park and particularly the Lido (S317)

5   Promote the long-term sustainability of the Lido.
6   See the Lido offers an ambience and balance of activities suitable for those of all ages, gender, diverse cultural backgrounds and life styles. [43]

What gave these criteria authority was the fact that a wide range of local bodies – Friends of Brockwell Park, Herne Hill Forum, as well as BLU – endorsed them in well-attended meetings.

In Paul Harvey (L29), the Lido found a knowledgeable council official who was able to make a huge difference. Contract Development and Strategy Manager for the Department of Environment and Culture at Lambeth Council, Harvey was the officer responsible for finding a future for the Lido that did not depend on Council funding. It was his survey in 2001 on health & safety work of £100,000 that needing doing that gave urgency to the issue: "The general thing was that the Council wanted it to be sustainable and the community wanted to keep the atmosphere and ambience and community spirit. Given that Lidos do not make money we were looking for a cash cow to sustain the Lido."

The process "was extremely difficult", Harvey says. For him, the biggest single tool to ensure that the ambience and community spirit survive is the Community Service Agreement (CSA): "It is a very strong document which allows Lambeth and the steering group to monitor what the contractor is doing, how he is doing it, why he is doing it."

He takes great pride in ensuring "that the people that I am dealing with, the ratepayers of Lambeth have their say, are democratically represented".

In 2002 May, Lambeth Council sent out an invitation to express interest,[44] followed by an invitation to tender. The crux of the Council's proposal was paragraph 4.1: "The Council is seeking a partnership arrangement from an experienced leisure developer and management operator. It is anticipated that a fully repairing and maintaining lease on the site of the proposed health and fitness facility [at – the document says 'and'] the Brockwell Park Lido will be granted for a minimum of 25 years, commencing in the autumn of 2003."

Of the 30 requests for an information pack, five tenders appeared, ending in a shortlist of three. The Lido Steering Group was involved at all stages of the process, including the choice of the organisation to kick off the next 70 years of the Lido.

The final three options, put to a public meeting on 2003 February 15, involved very different approaches: Baylight was a property developer proposing a second storey on the Lido and a three-storey 'Wellbeing Centre' in the car park at an estimated £6 million; Fusion was a not-for-profit leisure company that proposed a "glazed cloister" within the Lido including a 'Lifestyle Centre' whose subscriptions would help subsidise the pool, at an estimated £2.25 million; while Whippersnappers proposed a community trust/charity to run the Lido, refurbishing existing facilities (including converting the changing room block – called 'the pavilion' in the summary – for rent to a nursery and to community groups to provide income for the Lido), at a cost of £430,000.

Again, BLU circulated its 1000-plus members details of the three proposals ahead of the public meeting. "In the end," Mary Hill said, "we had looked at all the options. We knew Lambeth wasn't going to ride in and give us funding and we hadn't had a stampede of people wanting to run it, so we knew what the choices were."

ESCAPE The over-riding thing I remember is the blueness of the water, the vividness of it... that is a fantastic contrast to London and being in a big city which tends to be grey and colourless… At Brockwell Lido there is this wonderful vividness of the colours which are very uplifting in themselves.
– Janet Smith (L52)

Escaping from the rigours of urban life (S44)

Unhappy as I haven't got a garden, so the Lido gives me and my family the chance of some freedom, with the added benefits of all the extras (S45)

Fusion was the final choice. First, it was the only one of the three bidders with the experience of running pools. It was felt it offered "a reasonable opportunity for user and local representatives [to] be included in the supervision of the Lido". Finally, its approach of building an all-year-round leisure centre that could cross-subsidise the pool in wet summers was thought to be the one best able to guarantee long-term financial sustainability at least damage to the ambience of the Lido.[45]

Fusion founder and director Peter Kay (L36) said that when the invitation to tender arrived on his desk he didn't think it would be something to interest Fusion, but – "never say never" – he decided to at least make a site visit before finally deciding. It was a glorious day, the Lido full of people enjoying themselves and reminding Kay of his childhood visits to Sandford Parks Lido in Cheltenham, Gloucestershire (1935, still open). "That's what clinched it. We decided we could make it work, that we would put in a bid."

There is far from the cup to the lip, as the French say. Similar to the disputes between LCC and Lambeth of old, Fusion and Lambeth Council, with BLU looking on as an interested observer, got involved in long legal discussions about roles and responsibilities. Lambeth officer Paul Harvey describes it thus: "The biggest problem was when we had solicitors and started talking about leases and the community service agreements [CSAs]. There were hard-nosed people on either side. It did take a long time. What came out of if was a useful document which will not have to be rewritten if someone else does a similar thing elsewhere. It was almost like giving birth." He still feels it was a significant achievement: "We are breaking new ground [in the Fusion deal] – as a concept it is new

and we were a trail-blazer so there are always problems with that."

But all that looked a miracle of brevity compared with execution of the key element of the Fusion proposal: construction of new leisure facilities within the Lido complex.

First, in 2003 June, the original design, a glass corridor in the pool surround, was thrown out by English Heritage when the Lido – thanks to a campaign by the Herne Hill Society – got Grade II Listed Building status. PTEA, appointed as architects to implement the glass corridor in the very week of the Listing, had to go back to its drawing-board. English Heritage approved PTEA's new idea – of extending the south façade of the Lido six metres into the park (a "Tardis" idea, says PTEA lead architect for the Lido project, Jo Edwards (L22): "from the outside it's hardly changed but from the inside you've got lots more space") – as did a public consultation exhibition in 2003 October 20-26 (the flyer optimistically announced "Spring 2004: Construction period").

By the end of 2003, the project had both Planning and Listed Building consent. "It was extremely quick," says Edwards. "There was huge political will to get the project going and make it work." Mary Hill says: "The miracle was, because we were all sitting round that table, going through this time-consuming process, when it finally went for planning permission, there were no objections." Lido manager Rob Pagano (L46) came to the BLU AGM in 2005 and said work would begin at the close of the season.

But a problem reared its head – right where the proposed extension to the Lido was to be built there was, with poetic justice, a major water main: "It supplies half of south London, taking water to

Photo: Yvonne Levy

the Honor Oak Reservoir", said Jo Edwards, "so that had to be diverted". Negotiations with Thames Water about moving it were protracted and the cost – £100,000 – "almost scuppered the whole project", said Pagano. To add insult to injury, around Christmas 2005, a zealous official at Lambeth said that the modifications to the plan made as a result of accommodating the water main meant that the Lido project had to re-submit its planning application. "If it had, it wouldn't have been built," says Mary Hill. "It would have gone, that would have killed it." Fortunately, planning consultant David Taylor had just joined the steering committee.

He had worked for Lambeth and knew the ropes and was able to untie the Gordian knot.

In the meantime, for the three summers 2004–2006, there had been a transition period, where old and new regimes co-existed, with Paddy and Casey providing lifeguards, food and plant maintenance and Fusion administration, office staff and future planning – perhaps at times uneasily, but ultimately effectively in delivering to the public a swimming season and year-round classes.

At the end of the 2006 swimming season, work finally began. First, a solid marquee was erected on the café side, so yoga and other classes could

Bestival party at the Lido, , Sunday, 2006 August 13. This was organised by 'Rob da Bank'. Acts included the Laundrettas Swim Team and a Hip Hop and Reggae Greek Plate-Smashing Band.
Photo: Garret Keogh

continue right through the construction works. Phase one was the moving of the water main and then the Lido expansion itself. As the Thames Water project overran, the Fusion project was split into two stages: the first, to get enough work completed safely (ie without building debris) to open the summer 2007 season on time; the second stage, with builders working behind screens while swimmers cavort, the creation of the new fitness centre, due to open in autumn 2007.

If it is all completed to deadline, it will have taken a year – slightly less than it took to build the Lido in 1937.

It has been interesting watching the work progress from the eyrie of my tower block – moments of stillness followed by great spurts of activity. Torrential rains made the temporary path treacherous until the builders gravelled it. Winter winds blew down the proud placards inclusively naming all parties involved (unlike the 1937 one omitting to mention Lambeth Council).[46] And for the whole period, the dry pool has lain, awaiting its water, with a symbolic red boat beached on its bottom, pointing up the Park to the old lake where this all started, ready to transport us into the next 70 years...

The 1990s Lido – Sammy Dangerous

Sammy Dangerous (L69) walked through the Lido door just because it was open – soon after Paddy and Casey took their lease in 1994. After days of going, being told to leave and returning, he was given a job – and worked there for 13 years. For a couple of seasons he was there 24x7: "I mean every minute, every hour of every day from the 4th of May to the 15th of September. I work in the day in the cash office and I work at night in security. So I don't go home. I stay there for the whole season."

For him, "the Lido is a special place you know, it is not only me know that, everybody knows that. Lambeth knows that, the government knows that. It is different from all Lidos. I went to Charlton Lido the other day, it is rubbish, Tooting Bec Lido – none of them can compare to Brockwell Lido. It is a special Lido."

What makes it special for Dangerous is the people coming from all over London and beyond – and the standard of behaviour, all according to Lido rules. In his stress on discipline, Dangerous is very similar to Marlene Devaney (L65 – see Chapter 3) in the 1950s: for both, across 40 years, the Lido works best when the staff keep order amid the chaos of a hot summer's day: "I worked at reception for six years and at the front, at the gate, meeting all the people, the kids, boys, girls, everybody, I meet them. I know the trouble-makers; I know the good-behaving kids; I know everybody. Sometimes I have to ban them. It's not nice banning kids from coming in but sometimes you have to do it in order for them to learn and to have some discipline. For there is one thing we have to maintain at Brockwell Lido is discipline. We don't mind about rude boys or bad boys – when you come to Brockwell Lido you maintain the law and the order and the rules and the regulations of Brockwell Lido – and if you don't – you get a ban. Simple."

He banned a boy for pushing a kid in and the very next day saw him as bold as brass back in the pool – "and by the time I rush I don't know where, he turn and until today I didn't catch him and I don't know if he dived under the water and I was saying to myself, if he dived under the water, how long can he dive under the water? I waited and I still didn't see him – for the whole day and when we close, that is when he was going out and he said – 'you saw me – you were looking for me and you couldn't find me'. I said, 'yes, you beat me'."

That exchange between cheeky local kid and staff trying to be firm but fair could have happened any time over the past 70 years – and long will it continue doubtless. Dangerous has a fund of stories, including locking in overnight a group of midnight skinny-dippers foolish enough to say to him, "you can't manage six of us, why don't you just shut up?" He saw almost no violence by night, but daytime was a different matter: "Guys tried to jump the barrier to come in and the life guard said no and the life guard said no and the guy beat him up. I've seen things like that."

He remembers the parties organised by 'Rob the Bank': "You meet a lot of people, good people, behaving people. Sometime Rob has straw dresses and straw skirts and both male and female will be wearing dresses made from straw and he has some balloons marked 'Rob the Bank'. His music is fantastic. He likes a mixture. He plays everything – so the chef would be dancing, the bar man would be dancing, the gate man would be dancing, the person collecting the money – me myself – would be dancing."

But one of the quintessential sounds of the Lido was Dangerous making his announcements over the tannoy – and thus to most of Herne Hill, willy nilly: "I used to do some acting in Jamaica and drumming so I said, yea I can do it, and the first year I start to do it – straight away the people love it. So everybody like the announcements about the birthday. They would come and tell me. Little boys when their friends have a birthday ask me to sing happy birthday. The first person who asked me to do it was Paddy's mum, Jean. She came to me one day. She came to me and said, "Dangerous, can you sing a happy birthday song to a little girl over there for me?" I said, "I don't know, mum." She says, "I know you can do it, Dangerous". And I said OK and from that day I have been singing Happy Birthday until today."

If there's hype about the new regime at the Lido, Dangerous hasn't bought into it: "Well, to tell the honest truth, I was not in favour of this demolition, extension and gym and things like that. I think if it is a 1937 building I wish it was and stayed a 1937 building. I think people like it for what it was. I am not quite sure about the future right now. Because in the gym you are going to have machines that people are going to walk on and machines that people are going to ride on but they are riding to nowhere, and the walking machine is walking to nowhere. Why would you sit on a machine looking at a big wall in front of you in a park such as Brockwell Park that you could buy a cycle and cycle around the park saying hello to the girls, saying hello to the people in the park, looking at the birds, plants, looking at everything? Brockwell Park is a special park."

Timeline 4 – From 1994 Re-opening to 2007

1994 Paddy Castledine and Casey McGlue win seven-year lease to re-open Lido / Nigel Gilderson starts yoga classes; Caroline Burghard starts children's classes 1995 Modern Times documentary, *The Lido* 1996 Lido hosts LIFT party to celebrate Berthonneau fireworks event 2001 BLU – Brockwell Lido Users – set up. Gets 800+ Survey returns / Lambeth commissions consultants to report on Lido options 2002 **JANUARY** Lambeth open meeting to discuss consultants report. Steering group of six appointed **MAY** Lambeth asks for declarations of interest and then tenders to manage from prospective Lido-management consortia **JULY** 'Sink or swim', *Guardian* article by John Cunningham, on threat to Lido **DECEMBER** Steering Group meets Council re finalising bid 2003 **FEBRUARY** Fusion chosen as preferred Lido manager **JUNE** Lido listed Grade II. English Heritage rejects original 'glass corridor' scheme. PTEA, newly-appointed project architects, comes up with plan to extend south façade six metres into Park **OCTOBER** Open afternoon to discuss plans for refurbishment **DECEMBER** Planning and listed building consent 2004–2005 Legal discussions and negotiations with Thames Water over diverting of water main out of direct path of new extension. Christmas planning application panic. 2006 Work begins on water main and on Lido extension 2007 Planned re-opening, in two stages: Pool in July, Fitness Centre in autumn

by the side of the pool – Harry Eyres

by the side	of the pool
a pair	of ducks
female	and male
one pace	apart
no more	no less
beaks neatly	tucked
inside	their wings
take in	this sun
this blessed	sun
this sudden	blast
of mid-March	sun

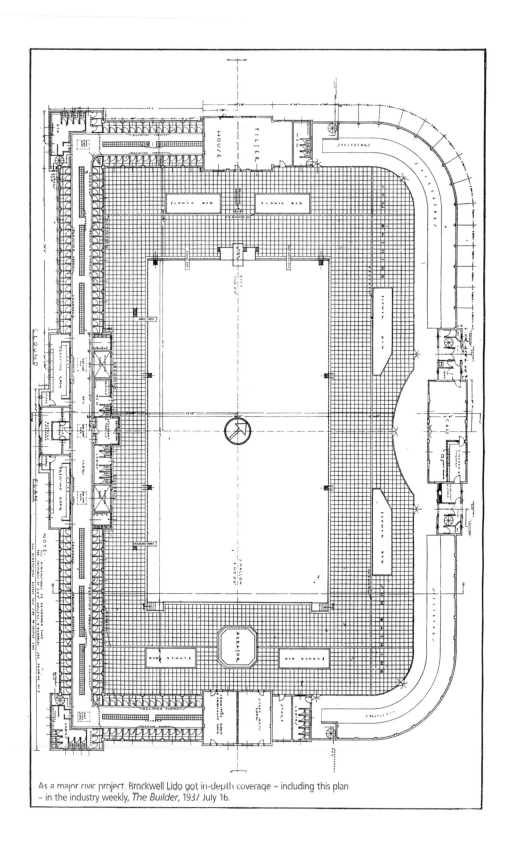

As a major civic project, Brockwell Lido got in-depth coverage – including this plan
– in the industry weekly, *The Builder*, 1937 July 16.

Chapter 5

Chapter 5

Architecture: Building and re-building of the Lido

'It had that sort of modern look about it. You felt you were going somewhere modern.' – Graham Gower

Directions: for convenience, the façade facing Dulwich Road will be called the North, that facing the Park, the South; East is the Shallow end, West the Engine Room/Deep end.

As a major civic project, Brockwell Park Lido got generous treatment in the construction industry weekly, *The Builder*. Its 1937 July 16 issue gave two pages and a column to the new pool.

The first page of its coverage shows a photograph of a landscape view of the Lido, taken from the south-east corner, with a flower bed and the octagonal aerator fountain to the right and the main diving board at the deep end to the left. Trees and houses in Dulwich Road can be glimpsed over the wall.

Underneath the photo were two sectional drawings of the design: a cross-section looking to the deep end and a longitudinal section looking to the café façade. The cross-section shows in a broken line the original slope of the terrain. Although the LCC supposedly chose the site for its flatness as much as its capacity to accommodate a pool "with amenities", the difference in level from highest to lowest points was, judging by eye, maybe two metres, so that at one end ground had to be excavated and at the other filled in. You can get a sense of this today by looking at the level of the park on the southern side of the Lido – there's a definite drop, marked by the flight of steps from the main path to the (now former) main entrance.

The second page of *The Builder*'s 1937 report is a full-size ground plan of the design. It is fascinating to see from this how much has changed in 70 years – because, apart from the shell of the brick building, almost everything else is not as it was in 1937. Only the poolside toilets remained where they were in 1937 and ironically, they have been demolished in the 2007 extension.

I must emphasise that what follows is per the plan; perhaps in reality the practical arrangements were different.

Looking first at the pool and its immediate surrounds, the shallow end at 2'6" and the deep end at 9'6" retain their founders' profundity. But all the diving boards, three at the deep end and two on the southern edge of the pool, have gone, as have the 'aerator' fountain at the shallow end and its flanking rectangular flower beds. Cindy Afflict (L1) remembers the diving boards in the early 1970s, towards the end of their life: "High one and the middle and a lower one. I remember a friend diving in the shallow end and losing a triangle out of her front teeth." Chris Huntley, who practised his widths at the Lido in the 1950s, says he remembers a sign on the 15 foot high diving board that was used in those days, which said 'no pissing' >89

Building of the Lido in 1937 (David Roy Hamley (L28))

Born in 1928, and living in Dulwich Road near the Lido ever since, David Roy Hamley was nine when the Lido opened. What makes his contribution so valuable is that he had a career in building and building education, with special expertise in brick – the Lido's main material. In 1946, he was apprenticed to Higgs and Hill, local building and civil engineering contractors. After National Service in the Suez Canal Zone, he achieved a First Class Full Technological Certificate in Brick Work in 1955 and a Teacher's certificate in 1958. He taught at Tulse Hill School and then was Senior Lecturer in Brickwork and Construction Technology at Vauxhall College of Building and Further Education.

Here's his account of how the Lido was built in 1936-37:

"They dug it by hand and the Irish navvies – I suppose they were Irish – wore corduroy trousers and they used to pull them up with a little tie like the coalman used to do and made them a little bit short around their ankles. And they would be digging this out and they wheeled the spoil, the stuff they had excavated, over to a place just about where you go into the car park from the park today (*he pointed out a spot on the southeast corner nearest the 2006 women's changing rooms*). There used to be a little park keeper's lodge there at the bottom of the gate and it was near there that they had this heap of stuff and it was all taken away by horse and cart. I don't remember it being taken away by lorry.

"It was all hand dug and then the building work started and the bricklayers came and it seemed to go very quickly. I understood from my father that it was piece-work brickwork and they had to do so much a day and it was built very quickly."

David went with interviewer Mary Hill to look at the brickwork– both the original brickwork and the new brickwork. He said the original bricks were 'Dorking Red' from the Dorking Brick Company (they're stamped 'DBC') – semi engineering bricks, dense and very durable. "These were hand-made and cut with wire. They were laid to give a multi-coloured effect. Several different colours were used. The different colours were achieved by varying the length of firing time. When the bricks were laid the builders stacked the bricks in piles of different colours and if they were stacked correctly the bricklayer would achieve a good mix of colours."

He criticised the modern laying of the vertical bricks at the top of the building – a crucial part of the quiet design of the Lido. In the 1930s, these were laid to be flush at the bottom, with mortar smoothed at the top to give a level appearance, while the 2006-2007 bricklayers had laid them to be flush at the top – "all wrong" to his eyes!

He mimed for his interviewer Mary Hill the felling of a large tree in 1936 which he had observed when he was watching the site being cleared in preparation for the Lido.

Modernism

Several people remark on how the Lido feels 'modern', remarkable in a building of that age... but this was the aim of the architects of the period – a new Modern style for a new modern age... even though it is in brick which was not a modern material and did not chime with those calling for a hard-line Modernism which would have involved just steel, concrete and glass. The use of brick was an English take on International Modernism, based on the 'soft' Swedish interpretations of the style as developed by a number of well-regarded Scandinavian and Dutch architects in the 1930s.

The Lido would have been designed from its function as a public pool, rather than from a pre-conceived notion of a suitable historic style. Hence its somewhat bare and stark appearance. It was designed, rather, from the inside, out. Any decoration would come from the use and the colour of the materials and the way they were arranged. Added decoration was seen as superfluous and Victorian. What mattered was its efficiency in doing its job.

It came out of the same impetus as the new Tube stations (eg Sudbury Town, 1931 and Northfields, 1932) being built on the extension of the Piccadilly line by the architect Charles Holden under the aegis of Frank Pick, Director of the London Passenger Transport Board.

Kate aan de Wiel, architectural historian

The Lido in 1939 April, with aerator fountain working. The only 1937 drinking fountain is extreme left of picture.

Building of the Lido in 2007 (Jo Edwards)

A crucial part of Fusion's vision for the long-term future of the Lido is to create new facilities – gym, spa etc – to generate revenue all year round and cross-subsidise any losses the pool might make in a wet summer. The existing space being too small for the new facilities, some new building was essential.

But what type of building? There was a strong feeling that the exterior of the Lido could not be touched. Ergo, any extension had to be built inside. A plan – inspired by Rick Mather's "glass cloister" 1999 Extension to an even more iconic local building, the Dulwich Picture Gallery – was drawn up to build a similar glass corridor inside the Lido, against the inner walls, giving Fusion the space it needed for revenue-generating gym space, while outwardly not altering the Lido's face to the Park. It was hoped that building it in glass would lessen the impact of the loss of the historic Lido inner space.

After a falling-out with the original builder, Fusion hired a new contractor, Cosmur, and a new firm of architects, Pollard Thomas Edwards Architects (PTEA), to build the glass cloister. But in the week PTEA's Lido project architect Jo Edwards (L22) started work, English Heritage lobbed a gigantic spanner in the glass cloister: it gave the Lido Listed Building Grade II status.

The listing of the Lido was a result of an initiative by the Herne Hill Society and the effort of Lambeth Conservation Officer Edmund Bird who suggested that the Society write to English Heritage, said Sheila Northover (L45). But the whole point of the listing was to preserve that wonderful inner space of the pool itself, designed for sunbathing and spectating. English Heritage officer Malcolm Woods took the view that the space around the pool was the thing that ought to be protected; and that the glazed corridor took away inner space and radically changed its look – it had to go.

Jo Edwards saw his point, coming out with the classic, "glass is not that see-through". There are reflections, for instance, and, she adds: "It makes a huge difference to put glass in front of something…" But "it made it more interesting for us that the first thing we had to do was start afresh".

She said: "We came up with five options and sat in a meeting with English Heritage's Malcolm Woods and he went through our book saying, 'No. No. No. No. Yes! I like that!'" What he liked was the idea – the brainwave of PTEA director Steve Chance – of taking down the Lido's south elevation and re-building it another six metres into the park, effectively doubling the width of the south wing: "It makes the building into a Tardis so that from the outside it's hardly changed but from the inside you've got lots more space. Fusion gets the space to put in the activities that make it financially viable, but from the park and the poolside it doesn't look as if the building's changed that much."

It was a bold idea: "It had just become a Listed building and we were talking about demolishing quite a large part of a Listed building, a very unusual approach." She says English Heritage was pushing her to be more radical, even more 21st century, but she resisted: "It was partly my own feeling of what was important about the building and its character – its amazing strong horizontality, and the verticality of the windows – and also a very strong feeling from so many people that they didn't want it to change. We were saying, let's change some little things in certain places to achieve interesting look-throughs and to make connections between the Park and the inside and the inside and the pool – but let's not make it look like a totally different building, let's keep it very much Brockwell Lido."

This decision was rooted in her view of the role of the architect: "What architects should do first is listen: listening to what people need or want and looking at and understanding what the site needs and could have." If listening to the building meant not radically playing with its 1937 character, listening to the people meant engagement with the many stakeholders – Friends of Brockwell Park, Herne Hill Society, Brockwell Lido Users, Whippersnappers, the yoga instructors, all embodied in the Steering Group – who had grown to have an interest in the Lido. It was a challenge but "it was a group of people who had been working on it a long time, really cared about it and probably realised it was not possible for everybody to have 100% of what they wanted, there'd have to be a bit of give and take – and they were prepared to do that to make it work". As someone who has swum and done 'pregi-yoga' at the Lido, Jo knows of what she speaks… The hard work with the community paid off – planning consent was achieved in record time without opposition.

A guiding principle was keeping true to the spirit of the Lido: "You want the existing character to remain clear and strong but it's also important that what's added is also clear. So there's a simple glass slot between where the old Lido finished and the new extension starts. In another 70 years' time that will be an important part of the building's history, that it was extended in 2007 – and these are the new bits and these are the older bits."

David Hamley would appreciate her comment that "the brick took a long time to get agreed. That is a very expensive brick (£700 per 1000, as opposed to £200-£350 normally). Because they're hand made they have a lovely texture and it's very difficult to find bricks like that these days. It's such an elemental building, with very few materials in it, and the brick is the main one. It had to be right."

She says a lot of people find the Lido's style rather dour and that it can take them a while to appreciate "a very elegant building. One of the things I like about the Lido is that it appears to be symmetrical but is not totally symmetrical: it plays with symmetry. A lot of people don't realise how good the architecture is because it's very understated. Simplicity but eloquence is its strength – it makes the right moves in the right places to tell you where to go and it doesn't shout about it. The old entrance didn't shout 'entrance', it was just obvious that that was where you had to go." She hopes she can achieve that clarity in the new design. One challenge is that the new main entrance is moving from the south to the east: "It's quite hard to drag people round the corner and make it clear that the entrance is now around there."

She finds creativity in working with an existing building: "You're reacting to something already there, which can be more inspiring than having a blank slate, it's a different kind of challenge." Time will tell whether she's met it…

The 1957 LCC Swimming Championships: record number of nearly 600 entries. Finals (Brockwell Park, July 27) were marred by rain. Fourteen championship records created, including by Judy Grinham and 13-year-old Brian Phelps (later, Olympic bronze diving medal, Rome 1960).

Photographer unknown. Reproduced by kind permission of London Metropolitan Archives.

<83 although he claims he's not sure that he didn't imagine it – they certainly used to joke about it while diving off. The Lido was invaluable to his brother who had polio: his mother Mary refused to let him stay inactive – "lots of swimming and walking around meant he retained the use of his legs which otherwise would have surely been lost".

At the deep end in 1937, between the diving boards and the filter house, two rectangular flower beds, slightly bigger than those at the shallow end, and a drinking fountain between them, have gone the way of all flesh. On the north side of the pool surround, two flower beds either side of the café,

rectangular but for a diagonal indent to echo the curve of the spectators' barrier, have gone too.

The northern poolside is designated for 'sun bathing'; and a barrier – pierced at seven points, presumably by lockable gates – separates it from curved tiers for spectators on each side of the café. On the north façade, each side of the café, was a spectator entrance, with turnstile and 'pay office', for galas. At each end of the curved arms of the spectator area there was a turnstiled spectators' exit, protected by a brick wall, so outsiders couldn't see into the Lido. Spectator toilets were beside these exits (women at east end, men at west end). >92

Lido Details, 1937

Total area: 2¼ acres   Pool: 165ft long x 90ft wide   Capacity: 600,000 gallons

Construction cost: £26,000; most (£24,000) paid by Metropolitan Borough of Lambeth; remainder by London County Council

Architects: HA Rowbotham ARIBA and TL Smithson LRIBA, LCC Parks Department

Shallow end: 2ft 6in.   Deep end: 9ft 6in.   Café: 50ft x 20ft

Diving boards: one 5-metre diving board; 3-metre fixed and spring boards; 1-metre fixed and spring boards.

Special feature: 'scum trough' at deep end – continuous withdrawal of top water to a depth of 12in. Could filter whole pool in five hours.

Main contractors: G Percy Trentham Ltd, 63 New Oxford Street, London WC1

Sub-contractors: East Anglian Cement (hydraulised hydraulic lime); Leeds Fireclay (glazed brickwork); Dorking Brick Co (facing bricks); Girlings Stone (synthetic stone); Crittalls Manufacturing (metal windows); British Reinforced Concrete Engineering (reinforcing fabric); Ruberoid (steel roofdecking); Ten Test Fibre Board (ceilings); Linolith Flooring (composition flooring in café); Milner Safe (lockers); Chas Wicksteed (diving stage, chutes etc); Smith's English Clocks (electric clocks); Sir WH Bailey (turnstiles); Tarmac (pre-cast paving slabs); United Filters & Engineering (filtration plant); NW Mitchell & Sons (expanding (cork) jointing); Dale's Lettering (lettering and depth marks); Granitese (seamless cement wall glazing).

Lido Details, 2007 Extension

Total area of extension: 1471 sq mtrs   Construction cost: £2,725,000

Client: Fusion   Funding facilitator: Alliance Leisure

Architects: Pollard Thomas Edwards. Lead architect Jo Edwards, assisted by John Yeudall. Director in charge: Stephen Chance. Interior design and brand strategy: Revolution Design.

Main contractors: Cosmur Construction Ltd, 72 Salusbury Road, London NW6 6NU

Sub-contractors: 24 Hour Heating Services – Plumbing; ADB – Painting; Barking Brickwork – Brickwork; Barwins – Brick repairs; Byford Interiors – Ceilings; Caledonian Glass and Glazing – Frameless glazing; Caledonian Glass and Glazing – Glazing; Central Diamond Drilling – Concrete Cutting; Cheshire Spas and Pools – Hydro Pool; Clements Windows – Metal windows; Connolly Demolition – Demolition; County Construction – Canopy; County Construction – Steelwork; CWC Flooring – Flooring; DBS Scaffolding – Scaffolding; Dynamo Site Services – Labour; EAS – Asbestos Removal; Emmerson Carpentry – Carpentry; Fitch Flooring – Flooring; Hanover Electrical – Electrical; Harrow Plumbing – Plumbing; Hawkeye Security – Security; Helo – Sauna and Steam; Hill McGlynn – Labour Hire; I Tab – Turnstiles; In Line Tiling – Tiling; JG Plastering – Labour; Metali Windows – Window Refurbishment; Metalwork – Surround to Turnstiles; Milbank Floors – Beam and block; NBS Bricks – Handmade Bricks; PCS Cabinets – Reception desk; PMC Foundations – Groundworks; RE Petit and Sons – Removal works; Rosslyn Plastering – Plasterers; Safespace Lockers – Locker and cubicles; Securec – Plasterers; Stewart Anthony – Mechanical and Ventilation; Tilbury Roofing – Roofing; Tony Conroy – Tree removal; UK Screeders – Screeding

A Lifeguard's Sense of Place, 2004

If you let it, you become aware that the whole site of the place, yoga rooms, café, operates as an altered mindset. When you go there, you are in the heart of the inner city, there is this bright blue open space surrounded by trees and beautiful redbrick walls that catch the light as it changes. Spending a day there is exactly like spending a day on the beach, the sunshine enters you and the water enters you, and the sensibility of the people you meet there alters you, affecting how you think and look at the world. Physical beauty of the place – the way it works, the way those walls reflect the sunlight, the water, the colour changes; the fact it's in a valley, the park rolls away above you. It does feel like a magical space that you enter through a wall. I love the sun; all my life, I associate sunshine with happiness and the Lido with happiness, and summers with happiness, and it's always the worst day of the year when it closes, and the best day of the year when it opens.

Howard Cunnell, senior lifeguard 2004

Photograph courtesy of Zoe and Rupert Burt

RELAXATION

Because the pool is not only a pool, you know, it's a place that people enjoy being. They come to sit and enjoy the atmosphere, enjoy it – just sit there and enjoy it. Just to sit by the pool I'm just enjoying myself, even if I'm not drinking, even if I'm not smoking, even if I'm not eating, just enjoying myself. Brockwell Lido is a very special place. – **Sammy Dangerous (L69)**

It's very relaxing and I feel like I'm on vacation for a few hours **(S286)**

<92 The café had a right-angled kitchen and serving hatch in its north-east corner, with scullery and store room to the east.

The west side had a filter house, as now, and the east side three quite small rooms, given the capacity of the Lido: Staff Mess Room in the middle, with Store to its north and Committee & Ambulance Room – much used for Galas – to its south.

But the real shock is on the south side, where almost nothing now is as it was in 1937. The biggest change of all is that the whole southern block of the building and the 'dog legs' at each end comprised one great open space (by 2006, before the Lido closed for refurbishment, this had been divided into a series of small rooms). 'Dressing Cubicles' lined the walls on both sides of this great space and lockers occupied its middle. As the Opening Ceremony leaflet informs us, there were 162 cubicles and 880 lockers – amazing provision. When full, this great space must have felt like a mainline station, though with less clothes. You can see with a space this large how a shift system could be operated on busy days.

The swimmers' entrance to the Lido was through the southern façade, facing onto the Park. When you came in, there was a small lobby, with a Pay office ahead of you, which had a paying window either side, presumably for men and women respectively, but no turnstiles are drawn on the plan here. As was the case until 2006, 'Ladies' went to the right and 'Men' (not 'Gentle' on this plan) to the left, as you come in from the Park. On either side of this paying area was a large dressing room, which I suspect was used for school groups – lockable and keeping the kids all in one convenient place.

Lambeth Archivist Graham Gower (L27) was taken for weekly swimming lessons (with PE teacher Mr Drinkwater) by his school to the Lido in the mid-1950s. He remembers the changing rooms as "dark and bitter and cold and dismal", although the actual swim was "a nice experience, bright and modern". Being skinny, he used to freeze and says that "when you got bored you went round the fountain [at the shallow end] and had a chat". The fountain was working but the school wouldn't let them play in it. Jean Phelps (L48) said the fountain in the 1940s was "out of bounds so far as the attendants were concerned but when backs were turned we loved to climb on it and feel the water rushing down from above". And one of the iconic images of the Lido – a 1948 one in the Frith Collection – is of the fountain positively overflowing with children.

At either end of this south block, the space in the angle contained toilets, beside which was the swimmer's exit.

Once you had paid, you left the entrance hall and came into a great lobby. You would see the line of lockers to left (men) and right (women). Immediately ahead was the Attendants & Towels office, with two counters facing you in the lobby and an Observation post facing the pool; this office occupied the small open space through which swimmers used to enter the pool until 2006 – the one marked poolside by the square clock. Parliament Hill Fields Lido – designed by the same architects – still has the same layout, with the lifeguard observation post facing the pool at this point.

Either side of the Attendants & Towels office were toilets, in the same place as in 2006 and, as then, only accessible from poolside. Strange to think that the only architectural spaces to survive 70 years were these two toilets and a bit sad for those of a

Photo: Miranda Payne

nostalgic bent to see them finally going.

Flanking each toilet was a wading pool, the only – and hygienic way – swimmers could access the main pool. Beyond the wading pool on each side, and quite small for the capacity of the place, was a room with 'Footbaths' and two Showers, accessible only on the changing room side – you had to wade through the wading pool first.

David Briggs (L9), born 1949, remembers the Lido of the 1950s: "You put all your clothes in a wire basket and you used to take them to a counter and they'd give you a rubber band to put on your wrist or ankle and I remember you used to have to walk through a pool of cold water."

Graham Gower's favourite word about the Lido, almost 20 years after it was built and despite it having gone through a war, was "modern": "It had that sort of modern look about it. You felt you were going somewhere modern. Streatham Baths looked a bit old-fashioned, the Lido was modern in most respects. Cheerful memories, really, bright and sunny, modern. Spacious. I have positive memories of it."

On the pull: the wedding of Zoe and Rupert Burt in 2003 September.

Appendix 1

Lido Book Interviewees

Code	Surname, Forename (Interviewer)
Code	*Surname, Forename (Interviewer)*
L1	Afflict, Cindy (self-written)
L2	Andrews née Mead, Joyce (Carolyn Weniz)
L3	Attree, Lizzy (Mary Hill)
L4	Austin, Jane (Yvonne Levy)
L5	Boyle, Michael (Hylda Sims)
L6	Burghard, Caroline (Peter Bradley)
L7	Burt, Zoe (Yvonne Levy)
L8	Butler, Robin (Peter Bradley)
L9	Briggs, David (Yvonne Levy)
L10	Cameron, Marcia (Yvonne Levy)
L11	Carter, Melody (Yvonne Levy)
L12	Castillo-Binger, E. Hilda (Hylda Sims)
L13	Castledine, Paddy (Peter Bradley)
L14	Castledine, Jean (Melanie Mauthner)
L15	Collins, Pat (Yvonne Levy)
L16	Cunnell, Howard (Miranda Payne)
L17	Irving, Violet (Hylda Sims with Dawn Henchy)
L18	Demetriou, Andreas (Mary Hill)
L19	De Montgolfier, Christiane (Peter Bradley)
L20	De Wend Fenton, Rose (Carole Woddis)
L21	Duffy, Paul (Mary Hill)
L22	Edwards, Jo (Peter Bradley)
L23	Eyres, Harry (self-written)
L24	Fensterheim, Helen (Carolyn Weniz)
L25	Gilbert, Jacqui (Yvonne Levy)
L26	Gilderson, Nigel (Mary Hill)
L27	Gower, Graham (Peter Bradley)
L28	Hamley, David (Mary Hill)
L29	Harvey, Paul (Mary Hill)
L30	Hill, Mary (Peter Bradley)
L31	Hoare, Theresa (Yvonne Levy)
L32	Holman, Judy (Peter Bradley)
L33	Holmes, Dom (Yvonne Levy)
L34	Hunt, Joan (Mary Hill)
L35	Huntley, Matthew (Mary Hill)
L36	Kay, Peter (Peter Bradley)
L37	King, Jack (Mary Hill)
L38	Legrice, Lily (Yvonne Levy)
L39	Levy, Crispin (Yvonne Levy)
L40	Levy, Yvonne (Peter Bradley)
L42	Malwa, Victor (Miranda Payne)
L43	McGlue, Casey (Peter Bradley)
L44	Mitchell, Rose (Yvonne Levy)
L45	Northover, Sheila (Melanie Mauthner)
L46	Pagano, Rob (Peter Bradley)
L47	Phelps, Thelma (Peter Bradley with Mary Hill)
L48	Phelps, Jean (self-written)
L49	Russell, Caroline (Judy Holman)
L50	Sas-Terlecka, June (Carolyn Weniz)
L51	Satyanathin, (Peter Bradley)
L52	Smith, Janet (Yvonne Levy)
L53	Spashett, Linda (Mary Hill)
L54	Steinger, Catherine (Mary Hill)
L55	Thackray, Becca (self-written)
L56	Thompson, Ruth (Melanie Mauthner)
L57	Thorpe, Siobhan (Carolyn Weniz)
L58	Tomiczek, Caroline (Mary Hill)
L59	Whelan, Clare (Mary Hill)
L60	Whitton, Douglas (Mary Hill)
L61	Williams, Julia (Mary Hill)
L63	Willoughby, Daniel (Miranda Payne with Mary Hill)
L64	Sims, Hylda (self-written)
L65	Devaney, Marlene (Mary Hill)
L66	Walters, George & Gray, Roddy (Kate aan de Wiel)
L67	Cowell, Irene Joan (self-written)
L68	Challen, Pat (Mary Hill, Dawn Henchy)
L69	Dangerous, Sammy (Mary Hill)
L70	Gillespie, Cheryl (Mary Hill)
L71	Hogarth, Susy (Mary Hill)

The 1955 LCC Championship finals at Brockwell Park July 23, held in excellent weather, were outstandingly successful. Among the large entry were several of the best swimmers and divers in the country. The fine weather meant LCC swimming baths and lidos had their busiest season since the war.

Appendix 2

London Swimming Championships at the Lido

1947 (1st year): The first County of London (LCC) Swimming Championships. Area swimming heats were held: south of the river, at Brockwell Park Lido on June 7 and north of the river, at Parliament Hill Fields Lido on June 21, with the finals taking place at Parliament Hill Lido on 1947 July 12.[A2.1]

1948 (2nd year): "The swimming championships were again popular and the standard of performances and the number of entries showed an improvement on 1947:" Finals Brockwell Park, July 24.[A2.2]

1949 (3rd year): Swimming championships "proved very popular". Entries, especially for the South area meeting at Brockwell Park, showed a considerable increase.[A2.3]

1950 (4th year): Finals Brockwell Park, July 15: "A very high standard was reached, 13 events producing new records."[A2.4]

1951 (5th year): By now the championships are described as "well established". 1950's "record entry" was beaten and "most of the winning times were better than last year". Expenditure £108; income £685.[A2.5]

1952 (6th year): "Many of the previous year's times were improved upon." Finals Brockwell Park, July 26. Expenditure £121; income £715.[A2.6] It was agreed to include diving into the Championships for the first time.[A2.7]

1953 (7th year): "Large entry and a high standard… A girls' diving event was held for the first time…" Swimming championships "enthusiastically supported by many well-known London swimming clubs." Expenditure £111; income £633.[A2.8]

1954 (8th year): Total entries for Swimming Championships of over 400. Finals Brockwell Park, July 17 "in very bad weather", included Southern Counties Water Polo finals. Races were run lengths, not widths, as previously and butterfly event added: "New trophies will be required."[A2.9]

1955 (9th year): "Held in excellent weather… outstandingly successful. Among the large entry were several of the best swimmers and divers in the country." 3500 spectators at the three meetings (finals – at Brockwell Park July 23 – and two area meetings). New records in 16 out of 20 events. Expenditure £170; income £785.[A2.10] The fine weather meant LCC swimming baths and lidos "had their busiest season since the war.[A2.11]

1956 (10th year): Record number of entries and 15 new records. "Overcast skies and pouring rain" marred the two Area Meetings on July 14 "for the few spectators who attended" Expenditure £812; income £75 (huge loss due to loss of revenue from spectators).[A2.12]

1957 (11th year): Record number of "nearly 600" entries and "standards of performance continue to

Four trophy winners in 1961.

Photographer Ron Chapman. Reproduced by kind permission of London Metropolitan Archives.

Photographer unknown. Reproduced by kind permission of London Metropolitan Archives.

COMMUNITY Cool clean water and friendly smiles to start the day; friends and strangers all meeting to relax and play together. A unique place to be proud of in Brixton (**S343**)

It is very important for the community, especially the children, that the pool is kept open as an open-air pool. It brings a lot of happiness (**S663**)

A good-feel factor and well-chilled and friendly atmosphere, with white and black, straight and gay people and families sharing the venue (**S675**)

The mayoral marquee…

rise". Area and Finals (Brockwell Park, July 27) meetings "marred by rain". Fourteen championship records created, including by Judy Grinham and 13-year-old Brian Phelps (later, Olympic bronze diving medal, Rome 1960; and Commonwealth medals 1958, 1962, 1966). Expenditure £740; income £112.[A2.13]

1958 (12th year): Record 542 entries, ten records broken. Olympic gold medalist Judy Grinham broke record at finals (Parliament Hill, July 12). Southern Area Meeting at Brockwell Park Lido June 28.

Expenditure £800; income £93. Spectator charges: Adults 1s (5p), children 6d (2½p).[A2.14] "As an experiment," a swimming coaching course was run at Brockwell Park Lido, in association with the Central Council for Physical Recreation (CCPR): "In spite of bad weather, pupils attended regularly and whereas at the start of the course none could swim, all could swim and dive – some really well – on completing their course of eight hourly lessons. We have had letters of appreciation from some of them."[A2.15]

They're off! Smoke from the starting pistol, 1963.

Photographer Ron Chapman. Reproduced by kind permission of London Metropolitan Archives.

1959 (13th year): Record 594 competitors at swimming championships, with 14 records broken. Fine weather, with 505 spectators at Brockwell Park Lido July 4 and 651 there for the finals, July 18. Championship expenditure £752; income £152. For a second year, swimming coaching was run at Brockwell Park Lido, and started at Parliament Hill Fields Lido; coaching expenditure £32; income £52.[A2.16]

1960 (14th year): Record 679 individuals and 55 teams in swimming championships, but "dull weather lessened number of spectators". Championship expenditure £90; income £100.

Swimming coaching again run at Brockwell Park and Parliament Hill Fields Lidos; coaches' fees were raised from 15s (75p) to one guinea (£1.05p) per hour.[A2.17]

1961 (15th year): Swimming championships "again well supported and their status is now very high". Finals Brockwell Park Lido, July 15. Championship expenditure £650; income £119.8s (40p). The Chief Parks Officer, LA Huddert, suggested to the Parks Committee that the swimming coaching should begin a week later in 1962, on June 4: "It is hoped that by not starting the courses until June the weather will be kinder and the water warmer in the

HAVEN/OASIS In 1994 I was living at that time with a man who was ill. He had AIDS. And the fact that that pool reopened, that I used to go there in the mornings and get rid of some of the tension and frustration by bashing up and down, it was really important to me. It was quite a lifeline at that time. – **Ruth Thompson (L56)**

open-air Lidos." Championship expenditure £130; income £107.5.0 (25p).[A2.18]

1962 (16th year): 700 individual and 60 team entries; 12 records set: "Several international swimmers competed… and the standard of swimming was very high." CCPR swimming coaching now extended to five pools, including Brockwell Park. Championship expenditure £595; income £106.10.6 (52½p); coaching expenditure £160; income £63.15.0 (75p).[A2.19]

1963 (17th year): Finals at Brockwell Park Lido, July 13; 13 new records.[A2.20]

1964 (18th year): This was the final year of LCC-organised swimming championships (finals, Parliament Hill Fields, July 11), as next year the LCC was replaced by the Greater London Council (GLC). In a valedictory, the LCC Parks Committee said "many individual sportsmen and officials… have expressed thanks to the Council [LCC] for promoting these championships. Since their inauguration they have become well-established and… held in high regard."[A2.21]

1965 (19th year): On April 30, the incoming GLC Parks & Smallholdings Committee (chair, Peggy Jay) issued a major report on the LCC Championships: They "served to draw the attention of the public to the recreational facilities available in the parks… [and] have established themselves in the outdoor life of London" – and the Committee proposed to continue them, renamed as 'The London Swimming Championships'.[A2.22] As before, area meetings were held at Brockwell Park and Parliament Hill Fields Lidos, but the finals were held indoors at the Crystal Palace National Recreation Centre on July 10, "a

transfer… popular with both swimmers and spectators…" Due to the GLC's greater catchment area, entries rocketed by 500 to over 1100 – "by far the most popular of all the sports championships". Miss Linda Ludgrove won the women's 110yds back stroke "and, only a fortnight later, broke the world record."[A2.23]

1966 (20th year): The surge in entries of 1965 was maintained in 1966, with over 1100 again participating. Both Area Meetings and Finals were in the Lidos this year, "although the weather was very bad".[A2.24]

1967 (21st year): Perhaps because of the bad weather the previous year, entries dropped to (a still respectable) 900. Area heats were again held in the two Lidos on June 24, though "bad weather marred them". The Finals were indoors in Crystal Palace on July 8.[A2.25]

1968 (22nd year): Numbers dropped again for the 1968 Championships, to 850 entries. For the last time, Area meetings were held in Brockwell Park and Parliament Hill Fields Lidos, on June 22. Then comes the killer sentence in the Parks Committee report: "For the third successive year these meetings were marred by bad weather and, following representations by swimmers and officials, arrangements are being made for these preliminary events to be held indoors at the NRC at Crystal Palace" – where they were duly held on July 6.[A2.26]

In **1969**, all phases of the Championships were held indoors at Crystal Palace and they never returned to the Lidos.[A2.27]

It was the end of an era.

The Brockwell Icicles club strut their stuff at 36 degrees Fahrenheit (2.2 degrees Celsius) in 1972. Photograph courtesy of Casey McGlue.

Appendix 3

Book Contributors

Peter Bradley: Out of the blue…

I could do a Christopher Wren and say, if you seek why I wrote this book, look around you. But that would be both wrong and cheeky, as this has been such a collaborative effort: so much of this book has been written by the interviewed and their interviewers. It has been a new experience for me to work with 70+ contributors. Weaving their words into my own, seasoning archival research – which I love – with the sweet and salt of living people's recollections, has been tough and rewarding. History is about the past but always also about the living, our take on where we are now, where we want to go. Down the years, I have loved Brockwell Park and its Lido and that has informed what I've done here – I hope to write a bigger work on the Park some sunny day. *Ad multos annos…*

Mary Hill: Why I am involved in the project

To me swimming is outdoor swimming – a feeling formed in childhood in a hot climate. In the mid 1990s I re-discovered the pleasures of open-air swimming at Brockwell, but found something more important – the Lido had its own sense of community – linking a diverse collection of people who had in common this shared out-door space, and a desire to escape the urban hustle. The Lido, both the pool and Tai Chi, made Herne Hill a better place for me. In summer 2001 I helped with a survey organised by Brockwell Lido Users (BLU) to find out what other people thought about the Lido. I was amazed at the response (873 returned questionnaires) and the strength of the feelings expressed. It was clear that the Lido was so much more than a swimming pool. The sense of community was mentioned again and again.

The BLU survey came about because in February 2001, Lambeth's health and safety report had found over £100,000 of repairs required before the Lido could open for the summer season. Although the Council found funding for essential work and the pool opened, in August there was no news about the future of the Lido. The seven-year lease of the Lido to Paddy Castledine and Casey McGlue was scheduled to expire before the next swimming season. Many users gave a phenomenal amount of time, energy and skills over the next six years to the Lido campaign.

Although many users would have liked for the Lido to stay very much as it was in 2001, something had to be done because Lambeth, like other local authorities, was not able to continue to fund outdoor swimming; it had to become self-financing. The deteriorating state of the buildings meant that the Lido could not continue long without investment. The BLU survey showed that it was not enough just to save the buildings and the pool, users were committed to the Lido because of its ambience – its sense of community. But try as we might in long meetings about legal documents it was difficult to set out what it was in this "ambience" this "sense of community" that we could define in a legal document. We could, however, obtain a commitment to give users and the local community a voice in how the Lido is run and what happens next. This was done in a Community Service Agreement which set up a Brockwell Lido Steering Group.

My hope is that this book will help to capture, in a way that legal documents cannot, what the Lido means to people and makes it part of their memories. If so, I think it will give us all a better understanding of how we can maintain and develop what people value – the Lido must pay its way but we must find ways to make that happen without sacrificing the fun and the sense of community ownership. The campaign to save the Lido does not end with a lease and a refurbishment.

Judy Holman

I wanted to be involved with the book celebrating the Lido's 70th birthday because I love it and therefore think it needs celebration. And I love the Lido because:

- I love swimming outdoors and I get brilliant exercise this way, my breath and my body and therefore my mind becoming more harmonious and peaceful
- I love the way knowing that I can go to the Lido every morning means I have carried on through difficult times better than I would have if I couldn't
- I love being in the Lido first thing in the morning in touch with water, weather, sky
- I love seeing birds fly overhead and catching the glimpse of bright blue reflected in their wings as they pass
- I love knowing there will be someone to talk to who also loves the Lido
- I love the feeling of warmth I get when I walk into the Lido space

- I love feeling part of a group who is passionate about something
- I love the colour blue – it defines the Lido
- I love the others who use the Lido – families, children, beautiful people sunning themselves, widening the mix of people I come into contact with
- I love the look of the place – the space, the brick walls, the greenery, the banners, the trees over the top of the walls
- I love the feeling of connections – meeting people who have moved in and out of my life over the 30 years I have lived in Herne Hill

Yvonne Levy

I can't remember my first visit to the Lido. I know I must have said "Wow!" when I walked in and saw the glory of the pool but I did that every time I went. My idea of bliss is to be in the water on my own on a calm day, the water like silk. More playing than swimming. I can tolerate the odd duck or two but other human beings are not welcome, especially those splashy, wave-creating ones. This is a bit of a paradox when we all know that the future of the Lido depends on encouraging more users into the pool!

Lido, how do I love thee? Let me count the ways! The conviviality of the early morning swimmers, toast crumbs in the Marmite, wonderful Caroline dressed up as a crocodile at Whippersnappers, gorgeous lifeguards, pride when people pointed out my own son as one of them, barbeques and night swimming, hot showers to thaw the bones, happy families playing in the water, pride at my own grandchildren's swimming prowess, even more pride at my son's production of the *Blue Room*.

Enough, already! I wanted to be involved for the same reason that I wanted BLU to happen. I love the Lido and want it to be celebrated. This book is a wonderful way to do that. My Dad swam in the ponds before there was a Lido. I hope my granchildren will remember him and take their children and granchildren to the Lido. Here's to the next 70 years!

Hylda Sims: Saving the Lido

Once the Lido was just an ordinary a-political sort of place – the local open air swimming pool. Everywhere that was anywhere had one. Then, one by one, like previously unnoticed diamonds lying around on building sites, they began to disappear. Only very slowly, when they had nearly all vanished, did we realize that we were being robbed of our jewels, of something basic and beautiful, something we could live in: sky reflected in water.

How did this come about? After all sky and water are most of what we need when you come down to it… well… there were the people who, shut up in their council offices, had forgotten sky needed water, water needed sky. An extravagance we can't afford, they thought. A nuisance, they thought. Something over which one has no control. An unprofitable juxtaposition. Who needs it? Trouble.

Then there were their sometime friends the entrepreneurs… People today don't need S & W (they couldn't bring themselves to use the words), they need Choice. And we shall choose the choice for them. Relaxation is a business opportunity with fabulous potential. What people need is leisure centres, sports complexes, shopping malls and other plastic pleasures of the consuming kind and we, at a special discount price of course, shall provide them. And all things shall be virtual save

for the occasional pumping of iron and the running machine. There's no need to get your feet wet and if you should want to take a dip it will be at body temperature so you won't notice you're in. If any of you guys need sky, why, watch a screen or take a plane. If you guys need water, hey, hop a jet to Torremolinos or somewhere else foreign. We will provide the jet, at a special discount price of course. Believe us, these are all the things you need and we shall persuade you to need them. Lidos are so yesterday!

And yes, most of us were persuaded, for what else was left to us? Only a shabby place in Brockwell Park where nothing was posh and people came in all shapes, sizes, ages and colours. And they spoke to each other about everything and nothing using their own voices and the word 'profitability' was not heard in all that divine, democratic rectangle of brick, concrete and water reflecting the sky. When you got in the pool your skin could feel it, your heart knew where it was, everything changed for the better. Okay, the water said, you're in now, bit of a shock, but all is well. And we saw that it was good.

So when they came round to steal that particular rough diamond, we decided not to let them get away with it. And, lo, the Lido shone and sparkled in the light of our determination as it had never sparkled and shone before in the days when we took it for granted. And it was a tiny step towards saving the world.

Carolyn Weniz

I first went swimming in the Lido when I started teaching in Brixton 25 years ago – a group of us from college would go for a free early-morning swim. I do not remember much about it, other than it always seemed cold and the surroundings not particularly conducive to hanging around (nor those of the Park either). This did not deter me. I had always been a swimmer, with much of my childhood and my early teens in the summer spent all day at the local outdoor pools in West Wiltshire.

However, for leisurely afternoon swimming and sunbathing I went to Kennington, until it closed. From 1987 until Brockwell closed, I did sometimes take my eldest daughter there, but again I do not remember it being that inviting.

I got involved when the Friends of Brockwell Park was formed to fight the setting up of an athletics track. Then in succession I got involved with a number of other campaigns relating to the park, such as fighting the attempts to close the One O'clock Club and finally getting signatures on a petition and lobbying the Council to reopen the Lido. By then I had three children and swimming in the Lido was a cheap alternative to going away on holiday.

From when it reopened until the present, the Lido has gradually become a more and more important part of my life in the summer. I have met up with many early-morning swimmers as well as staff, who have become good friends. But, I have also spent many leisurely hours there on hot days with my family. Some years it has been our main "holiday destination" and we have only as a consequence spent a few days away (usually at festivals). For the past two years my eldest daughter has worked in the Beach Hut, so that has also increased the Lido's importance as part of my family's summer life.

I wanted to be part of the project simply because my family and I have had so many enjoyable times there over the past 25 years. I also love the Park which the Lido is part of, likewise my children, who have spent a large proportion of their lives there.

Although not strictly in Brixton, the Lido is a reflection of the uniqueness of everything I love about Brixton: totally cosmopolitan, very friendly, laid back but also crazy at times. I come from the country, but cannot imagine leaving this area now. Contrary to popular opinion, there can be a real sense of community in urban areas and going to Brockwell Lido makes me feel I belong to a very special community.

Carole Woddis: Brockwell Lido – 70 years on

As a theatre journalist and reviewer for the past twenty or so years, my life has largely revolved around sitting in darkened rooms. As a resident for much of that time in Covent Garden, my sanity was preserved by swimming at the Oasis. At times this seemed magical: in the heart of the city, yet outside. At others, it was like being in the middle of the M25; 'manic' office workers jostling for space as they dashed up and down the lanes before going to work. You had to keep up!

When I moved south of the river, to Camberwell, for some time I was unaware of Brockwell Lido. A couple of years previously, it's true, I had been invited, as a member of the press, to an event organised by LIFT held at Brockwell Lido. But the penny hadn't dropped. Then, one hot day, I 'discovered' the Lido and my life was, in a word, transformed.

Suddenly there was space, cool water; there were big skies, on certain evenings there were

HAVEN/OASIS An outdoor oasis (**S24**). Feels like being abroad (**S42**).

An urban oasis (**S515**)

It's a little oasis amidst this stressful city. I love to relax by the water – very calming (**S112**)

Haven from outside world – my favourite place (**S134**)

It's a haven that is the only saving grace from a hot, stressful city (**S204**)

Haven in the middle of London (**S672**)

even barbecues at which, sitting back with a glass of wine in one hand, and some gentle tropical music in the background, I imagined myself a million miles away, on some Caribbean or Pacific island. And then there were the smiling faces. Friendship seemed on permanent tap at Brockwell. I'd never encountered anything like it in all the years I'd lived in London.

I was brought up on lido swimming in Nottingham in the 1950s. Many of them are gone now sadly, like elsewhere. But re-connecting once again with lido swimming, it seems one of the greatest gifts available to us in the privileged West.

Brockwell's magic is special and too important to lose. This book and the many people who have contributed to it on Brockwell's 70th anniversary is our way of communicating our joy and the joy it has given so many down the decades in the hope, in its turn, it may inspire many others to follow suit in the years to come.

Gethan Dick: Blueness

The three bluest things in my life are Brockwell Lido, the jellyfish tank at the Horniman Museum and my duvet cover.

Brockwell Lido is a living jewel, an unexpected ecstasy. The sight of it when I walk through the doors into its courtyard lifts my heart up into my throat. I seem to soar high above it in the moments before I dash my face into its shining surface. When you lie on the bottom and look up through its surface, the sky looks pale and uninteresting against the intense stinging aquamarine that surrounds you.

www.gethan.org
Extract from an article originally published in Attack!!!! 6 – Response: Leighton, published by Wes White who can be contacted at www.ecartilage.co.uk

Dawn Henchy

The craft and joy of interviewing: here's Dawn Henchy's poetic account of her time at an old folks' luncheon club…

Sitting and talking of water, one April afternoon…
Don't taste, just feel, just swim

As we move from taste to feeling
to memories of swimming,
as one, and then another calls out:
'My boys loved going there,' 'My boy…' 'My girls…'
'Oh, what times we had,'
there's one whose voice breaks.

Will tears or laughter come
as her parched memories crack open?

Eyes closed, she remembers
the war years and
swimming in the Lido
on the way to work.

Dive down, deep, deep,
don't taste, only feel.

Lithe and dappled, she is caught in that
early morning moment of absolute, unrationed peace
darting in and out of the sunlight,
water slipping over her like a new dress.
One stroke echoing another.
Her. The water. Her.
That 's all there is.

She laughs and shakes her hair free of the swimming cap,
rivulets run down each side of her face,
framed in damp curls.

She shakes her head again,
and a little flick of water
catches us all, making us gasp.
So cold. So pure. So present.

Sources

Throughout the book, there are two letter prefixes for people quoted:

- L – refers to the 70+ Lido interviews with named individuals, conducted in 2006-2007 with consent mostly by taped interview by members of the Oral History team, though some are done by phone or written by the person themselves. These interviews will be deposited in Lambeth Archives.
- S – refers to the 800+ people who took part in the BLU Survey in 2001. As participants were guaranteed anonymity, these are not named but referred to by their survey number.

BLU Archive holds many documents and photographs but is held privately at present. Please contact the Archivist via the BLU website: www.brockwelllido.com

A note on dates: this book adheres to the UN sequential system of dating: Year, Month, Day, so the 70th anniversary of the opening of the Lido is: 2007 July 10.

Bibliography

In alphabetical order, by author:

Boyle, Michael, 'Eau or Dough?', page 10, *Friends of Brockwell Park Newsletter* 15, October 1993
Bradley, Peter, *Ways in to Brockwell Park*, Lambeth Archives, 2006
Dixon, Ken, Effra: *Lambeth's Underground River*, Brixton Society, 1993
LCC Ceremonial Pamphlets, volume 11, *New Open-Air Swimming Bath, Brockwell Park, Ceremonial Opening on Saturday, 10th July, 1937*. LMA
Paul, Iain, MacDonald, David and Mitchell, Mary, *70 Years at Stonehaven Open Air Pool*, Friends of Stonehaven Pool, 2004
Rumble, Jeffrey, *A Brockwell Boy*, Herne Hill Society, 2000
Smith, Janet, *Liquid Assets – The lidos and open air swimming pools of Britain*, English Heritage, 2005
Smith, Janet, *Tooting Bec Lido*, South London Swimming Club, 1996
Wiltse, Jeff, *Contested Waters: A Social History of Swimming Pools in America*, University of Carolina Press, 2007
Microfilms of the *South London Press* and the *Brixton Free Press* are held by LAD, while many libraries hold online subscriptions to the *London Times*.

Archival sources

The two archives I worked in most while researching this book are:

- LAD – Lambeth Archives Department, Minet Library, 52 Knatchbull Road, London SE5 9QU
- LMA – London Metropolitan Archives, 40 Northampton Road, London EC1R 0HB

LAD holds Lambeth municipal records from 1890s on. LMA holds records for London-wide authorities, LCC (London County Council) and GLC (Greater London Council).

Film

The Lido, BBC 'Modern Times' series, director Lucy Blakstad, 1995

Images

Lambeth Archives Department has put most of its Lido images online at the wonderful www.lambethlandmark.com
London Metropolitan Archives assigns its Brockwell Park Lido images to three main boxes: SC/PHL/02/1083; SC/PHL/02/1084; and, for Rosendale School in 1894, SC/PHL/02/0213.
Patrick Harrison: www.patrickharrison.com
Francis Frith Collection: www.francisfrith.com
Private individuals

Glossary

LCC – London County Council; ruled London 1891–1965
GLC – Greater London Council; ruled London 1965–1988

MBL – Metropolitan Borough of Lambeth; local authority 1891–1965
LBL – London Borough of Lambeth; local authority 1965–1988
COPD – Chief Officer, Parks Department; principal LCC parks officer
B&CC – Baths & Cemetery Committee, MBL
LAD – Lambeth Archives Department
LMA – London Metropolitan Archives

Pounds, shillings and pence… (£sd)

To convert pre-decimal (ie before 1971 February 15) currency: one old shilling (s) = 5p; one old penny (d) = 0.42p (as there were 20 shillings or 240 old pence to the £). Old prices were written in the sequence 'Pounds, shillings and pence' eg £59.11s.6d. Using the conversion rate above, the 11s.6d (also sometimes written '11/6') = 57½p (11 x 5p plus 6 x 0.42p).

Converting, say, 1937 prices into 2007 ones is a little more complex. The closest is comparisons with 2002: see *House of Commons Library Research Paper 03/82, 'Inflation: the value of the pound 1750 2002'*, available online at: www.parliament.uk/commons/lib/research/rp2003/rp03-082.pdf

This *Paper* helps you work out the multiples for the years 1750–2002. The multiple for 1937 is 42, so the 2002 equivalent of the 26,000 paid for building the Lido in 1937 is: £1.092 million (26,000x42). Sample multiples below:

1900 – multiply by 75
1937 – multiply by 42
1950 – multiply by 21
1960 – multiply by 14
1975 – multiply by 5

GEORGE GROSE

8, New Bridge St., London, E.C.4
Phone: Central 5561.

LUDGATE CIRCUS

SWIMMING COSTUMES.

The **OLYMPIC SILK.** Records are broken in these costumes, surely a proof of their superiority to any other costume. Each costume is entirely hand-made and is tailored to fit perfectly. Costumes to special measurements can be made at the same price. **30/-**

The **PURE SILK,** a Costume of good value, can be recommended **21/–**

The **SPUR SILK,** Marvellous value, Navy only - - - - **10/6**

The **SPUR CASHMERE,** All-Wool Cashmere Costume, used by most leading Clubs. This costume is still by far the best costume for Club swimming. Used exclusively by the Hammersmith Ladies' S.C. Can be supplied in any colour. **5/6**

The **SPUR POLO,** strong Navy Cotton, self-bound for strength. Low cut arms. Specially made for Water Polo. **3/6**

POLO CAPS.

These Caps have passed the test of the S.C.A.S.A. Guaranteed to fit. Made in strong drill cloth. **7/6** set of 7.

FLAGS
complete with sticks, Regulation size, best Bunting - **5/-**

STOP WATCHES. George Grose Stop Watch, guaranteed for Polo or Race Timing. Side stop action - **25/-**

RACING SLIPS.

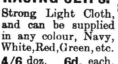

Strong Light Cloth, and can be supplied in any colour, Navy, White, Red, Green, etc. **4/6** doz.   **6d.** each.

POLO BALLS.

Improved SPUR, pneumatic, hand-sewn, best red leather - **24/6**

The Spur Buller, Ladies' Ball **23/6**

The Spur, No. 2, Pneumatic **21/6**

The Spur No. 3, Pneumatic **19/6**

TRAINING SUITS.

These Suits are similar to those used in the last Olympic Games. Essential to the race swimmer. Correctly cut and finished.

Can be obtained in colours— Black, Navy, Maroon, Royal, Green, White.

Zip Jacket	Zip Jacket
13/6	**18/6**
Elastic Ankles.	Zip Ankles.

SWIMMING GOGGLES - **7/6** each.

George Grose OLYMPIC Diving Boards.

14-ft., **£12 - 15 - 0**   16-ft., **£14 - 10 - 0**

The Official Olympic Spring Diving Board manufactured from selected Comb Grain British Columbian Pine and fitted with the Improved Rubber Cushion Fulcrum. Made to conform with all International requirements and to the specifications of the F.I.N.A.

Complete Fulcrum for Olympic Board   **£5 - 2 - 6**

1937 advert for swimwear. Notice the 'racing slips' – regulation wear under the swimming costume as essential protector of modesty. Multiply prices by 42 to get an idea of modern equivalent cost. the top 'Olympic Silk' costume would be around £63 today

Footnotes

Chapter 1: Swimming in the lake, 1890s–1930s

1.1   *LCC Minutes of Proceedings*, 1891 October 27, p1054. The *Minutes of Proceedings* are minutes of meetings of the full Council, but they often contain reports from various Council Committees, such as Parks & Open Spaces, for the full Council to take note of or vote upon. Obviously, the Committees met before the Council and so a Committee might meet on January 1 but its report be discussed at the full Council Meeting on January 15; my footnote references here are almost always to the full Council account of the earlier Committee report. This might be confusing! For instance, Footnote[1.3] below is about a Parks Committee meeting of 1891 November 13, but as reported in the full Council Minutes of December 8. Only very occasionally do I quote from the Committee rather than full Council Minutes.

1.2   A photo of this can be found at lambethlandmark.com

1.3   *LCC Minutes of Proceedings*, 1891 December 8, p1198

1.4   *LCC Minutes of Proceedings*, 1892 February 19, p179

1.5   *LCC Minutes of Proceedings*, 1894 May 8, p527.

1.6   In LMA photograph folder, ref SC/PHL/02/0213. Girls' photo ref: 79/260. Boys' photo ref: 95/022. They are part of an astonishing series of about 40 photos illustrating many aspects, scholastic and sporting, of the school.

1.7   *LCC Minutes of Proceedings*, 1894 October 23, p1033.

1.8   *LCC Minutes of Proceedings*, 1896 October 13, p1036.

1.9   *LCC Minutes of Proceedings*, 1896 November 17, p1266.

1.10   Smith, *Liquid Assets*, page 19, says that the trend to mixed bathing in the 1930s meant that men and boys "were forced to wear bathing costumes, which was seldom the rule in the single-sex Victorian swimming lakes". On p27, an 1899 photograph shows hundreds of naked boys bathing in Victoria Park lake, Hackney; hardly anyone is wearing a costume.

1.11   Article by WJ Perrin, 'The Glory of Brockwell Park – Have you seen the Liquidambar?' in *The Brixton Free Press*, 1920 May 28)

1.12   *Brixton Free Press*, 1920 May 7.

1.13   *Brixton Free Press*, 1920 May 28, 'The Glory of Brockwell Park – Have you seen the Liquidambar?'. He also states that there was "a fountain" near the lake.

1.14   *LCC Minutes of Proceedings*, 1898 July 26, p981.

1.15   At its 1900 January 19 meeting, the Parks Committee asked for an extra £100 because "owing to the very great use of the lake for bathing purposes, slightly more work will require to be done": *LCC Minutes of Proceedings*, 1900 January 30, p85. Tenders for Thames ballast at 6s6d (32.½p) a yard and Portland cement at £1.11s.10d (£1.59p) a ton were accepted by the LCC: *LCC Minutes of Proceedings*, 1900 March 13, p382.

1.16   *LCC Minutes of Proceedings*, 1901 January 29, p112

1.17   *LCC Minutes of Proceedings*, 1933 July 18.

1.18   *LCC Minutes of Proceedings*, 1900 July 17, p1007.

1.19   *LCC Minutes of Proceedings*, 1902 January 28, p114.

1.20   *LCC Minutes of Proceedings*, 1902 July 1, p1018.

1.21   *Brixton Free Press*, 1908 June 5: "Particulars to be obtained of the secretary or member of the committee."

1.22   *LCC Minutes of Proceedings*, 1902 July 1, p1018.

1.23   *LCC Minutes of Proceedings*, 1903 May 26, p897.

1.24   *LCC Parks Committee Minutes*, 1935 May 17, p143.

1.25   *LCC Minutes of Proceedings*, 1936 November 17, p435.

1.26   *LCC Minutes of Proceedings*, 1904 November 29, p2919.

1.27   *LCC Minutes of Proceedings*, 1905 October 31, p1419, reporting Education Committee meeting of October 25.

1.28   *LCC Minutes of Proceedings*, 1905 October 31, p1471.

1.29   *LCC Minutes of Proceedings*, 1908 March 24, p730.

1.30   *LCC Minutes of Proceedings*, 1910 July 19, p178.

1.31   *LCC Minutes of Proceedings*, 1911 November 28, p1302.

1.32   *LCC Minutes of Proceedings*, 1926 April 27-28, p761

1.33   *LCC Minutes of Proceedings*, 1928 December 4, p798.

1.34   *Brixton Free Press*, 1928 June 1, page 7.

1.35   *LCC Minutes of Proceedings*, 1929 April 23.

1.36   *LCC Minutes of Proceedings*, 1920 November 23, p860 – £550 "for cleaning out of lake"; LCC Minutes of Proceedings, 1930 December 16, p984: £885 for "mudding out ponds". At this period, 1930, 25 unemployed were working on the construction of Kennington Lido.

1.37   *LCC Minutes of Proceedings*, 1934 February 23, p57.

1.38   *LCC Minutes of Proceedings*, 1934 April 27, p97.

1.39   *LCC Minutes of Proceedings*, 1934 July 17, p172.

1.40   *LCC Minutes of Proceedings*, 1935 May 28, p768.

1.41   *LCC Minutes of Proceedings*, 1935 May 17, p154.

1.42   Rumble, page 10.

1.43   *LCC Parks Committee Minutes*, 1935 May 17, p154.

Chapter 2: Towards the Lido: The 1920s/1930s campaign for open-air bathing in Lambeth

2.1   LCC *Minutes of Proceedings*, 1923 March 20, p448

2.2   LCC *Minutes of Proceedings*, 1923 June 12, p840

2.3   MBL Council Minutes, 1927-8, p1085

2.4   MBL Council Minutes, 1929 January 28, p249

2.5   MBL Council Minutes, 1929 March 7, p453

2.6   MBL Council Minutes, 1929 May 27, p159

2.7   MBL Council Minutes, 1931 March 2, p84

2.8   MBL Council Minutes, 1934 January 1, p46

2.9   MBL Council Minutes, 1934 January 29, p54

2.10   MBL Council Minutes, 1934 January 1, p45

2.11   MBL Council Minutes, 1934 January 29, p61

2.12   MBL Council Minutes, 1934 September 10, p116

2.13   LCC Parks Committee Minutes, 1934 July 27, p205

2.14   MBL Council Minutes, 1934 September 10, p116

2.15   MBL Council Minutes, 1934 November 12, p144

ARCHITECTURE

Even though it's got a bit worn over the years it's still lovely. I'm a lover of old brick buildings anyway… it might need… sprucing up a bit. – **Marcia Cameron** (**L10**)

Original architecture (**S157, S218**)

A haven, the blueness, the old-fashioned quality of the place (**S16**)

We could use all the space. As children it seemed a very big space. We could run around and read a book and play games in the open air, go for a swim and it felt very uninhibited. It was an ideal space for children from 7 on. – **Susy Hogarth** (**L71**) who went to the Lido every summer day in the 60s

2.16	MBL Council Minutes, 1935 January 31, p279
2.17	LCC Parks Committee Minutes, 1935 February 15, p44
2.19	LCC Parks Committee Minutes, 1935 May 17, p154
2.20	LCC Parks Committee Minutes, 1935 May 17, p154.
2.21	LCC Parks Committee Minutes, 1935 November 22, p340-1.
2.22	MBL Council Minutes, 1935 June 3, p224.
2.23	MBL Council Minutes, 1935 November 18, p287.
2.24	MBL Council Minutes, 1935 December 2, p296.
2.25	MBL Council Minutes, 1936 March 2, p4.
2.26	LCC Parks Committee Minutes, 1935 May 17, p154
2.27	LCC Parks Committee Minutes, 1935 December 6, 354-5.
2.28	MBL Council Minutes, 1936 April 30, p575.
2.29	LCC Parks Committee Minutes, 1936 May 8, p107
2.30	LCC Parks Committee Minutes, 1936 May 22, p153; October 30, p229; and 1937 March 19, p73.
2.31	Interview L28. Hamley is particularly authoritative on the building of the Lido as he was in the building trade himself. See Chapter 5 on Architecture.
2.32	LCC Parks Committee Minutes, 1937 April 23, p113.
2.33	MBL Council Minutes, 1937 May 31, p123.
2.34	MBL Council Minutes, April 5, p107. The modern approach goes to the other extreme of Oscar Ceremony inclusiveness, with a panoply of boards on the embankment facing the Dulwich Road. 'Brockwell Lido – Investment, Improvement, Regeneration', says one. Principal funding partners Heritage Lottery, Fusion and Lambeth Council are mentioned ('delivered and part funded by Alliance Leisure') on other boards, as are builders Cosmur, architects, PTEA, interior designers and brand strategists Revolution Design.
2.35	MBL Council Minutes, 1937 May 31, p123.
2.36	LCC Parks Committee Minutes, 1937 June 25, p162.
2.37	Copies both in LAD (Ref: LBL/DAS/RL/1/2/5, pp14-15) and LMA (LCC Ceremonial Pamplets, volume 11; catalogued in date order).
2.38	Smith, *Liquid Assets*, page 26.
2.39	Tullio De Mauro, Marco Mancini, *Grande Dizionario Etimologico*, Garzanti Linguistica, Milan, 2000.
2.40	*The Times*, 1937 July 12, page 9C.

Chapter 3: 1937–93, from Opening to Closing

3.1	*Brixton Free Press*, 1937 July 16.
3.2	*Liquid Assets*, all of Chapter 2, pp18-25.
3.3	See Wiltse, Jeff, *Contested Waters*.
3.4	LCC Minutes of Proceedings, 1935 April 2, p452.
3.5	LCC Minutes of Proceedings, 1937 July 13, pp58-60.
3.6	*Times*, 1937 July 12, p9. Tony Blair's *eminence grise* Peter Mandelson is a grandson of Morrison.

3.7   *Times*, 1938 July 28, p12e, including photo. For under 12s only, it was 90ft square had a deep end of 3ft and a shallow end of 8in. The *Times* described it as "a very fine example of how the LCC looks after the welfare of its children".

3.8   For an account of the pool, see Paul, Iain, MacDonald, David and Mitchell, Mary, *70 Years at Stonehaven Open Air Pool*, Friends of Stonehaven Pool, 2004.

3.9   MBL Minutes, 1937 September 6, p131.

3.10   MBL Minutes, 1937 December 22, p194.

3.11   LCC Minutes of Proceedings, 1938 May 10, p573.

3.12   LCC Minutes of Proceedings, 1938 July 5, p25-6.

3.13   MBL Minutes, 1938 September 22, p1175-6.

3.14   LCC Minutes of Proceedings, 1939 February 21, p144.

3.15   MBL B&CC Minutes, 1939 March 27, p9. A photo of Guildford Lido c1933 in Smith's *Liquid Assets* (p20) shows almost every man in a full costume, while a 1938 one of Brockwell Park Lido in Bradley's *Ways in to Brockwell Park* (p17) shows almost every man in trunks.

3.16   MBL B&CC Minutes, 1939, p37.

3.17   Communication to Yvonne Levy. The ASA's 1937 Rule 58 on Competitors costumes stated: "Competitors in events held under ASA laws before audiences of both sexes, shall wear swimming costumes and drawers, or slips, except that, other than in diving events, drawers or slips may be dispensed with when the costume worn is of the skirt variety." Costumes had to conform to the following specifications: a. The material shall be cotton, silk, wool or any combination of such materials, provided the texture is non-transparent. b. cotton and silk costumes must be black or dark blue in colour, but bindings of club colours may be used. Wool costumes may be of any colour combination of colours provided that the colours do not make the costume appear transparent. c. They shall be of one piece, devoid of open-work, excepting above the waist at the back and side in the case of men and at the back in the case of women. All fastenings shall be on the shoulder. In the leg portion, the costume shall fit closely round the thigh. The skirt variety of costume is optional."

3.18   Rumble, p22.

3.19   LCC Ceremonial Pamphlets, volume 11, *New Open-Air Swimming Bath, Brockwell Park, Ceremonial Opening on Saturday, 10th July, 1937*.

3.20   LCC Minutes of Proceedings, 1939 May 23, p497.

3.21   LCC Minutes of Proceedings, 1939 September 22, p253.

3.22   LCC Minutes of Proceedings, 1940 April 30, p138.

3.23   LCC Minutes of Proceedings, 1941 May 20, p453.

3.24   LCC Minutes of Proceedings, 1942 April 20, p698.

3.25   LCC Minutes of Proceedings, 1943 April 13, p82.

3.26   LCC Minutes of Proceedings, 1944 April 16, p450.

3.27   LCC Minutes of Proceedings, 1945 May 15, p891.

3.28   LCC Minutes of Proceedings, 1941 May 20, p453.

3.29   LCC Minutes of Proceedings, 1942 October 20, p859.

3.30   See Bradley, p11-12, including photo, p11, of 1943 performance of *The Gondoliers*.

3.31   LCC Minutes of Proceedings, 1942 September 22, p816.

3.32   LCC Minutes of Proceedings, 1943 November 2, p270.

3.33   LCC Minutes of Proceedings, 1944 December 19, p715.

3.34   Elsie Turner (User ID: U536546), 'A Brixton Lass', from BBC WW2 archive, www.bbc.co.uk/ww2peopleswar/user/46/u536546.shtml

3.35   LCC Minutes of Proceedings, 1945 December 18, p1217.

3.36   LCC Minutes of Proceedings, 1944 May 16, p450.

3.37   LCC Minutes of Proceedings, 1944 May 16, p461.

3.38   LCC Minutes of Proceedings, 1945 May 1, p863.

3.39   LCC Minutes of Proceedings, 1946 April 5, p231.

3.40   LCC Minutes of Proceedings, 1946 May 28, p303.

3.41   LCC Minutes of Proceedings, 1947 January 28, p23.

3.42   GLC Minutes of Proceedings, 1965 May 11, p383.

3.43   LCC Minutes of Proceedings, 1947 June 13, p334; June 17, p356; July 17, p366.

3.44   LCC Minutes of Proceedings, 1947 November 4, p681.

3.45   LCC Minutes of Parks Committee, 1947 February 14.

3.46   LCC Minutes of Proceedings, 1947 October 21, p622.

3.47   *Times*, 1963 July 19, p4c.

3.48   LCC Solicitor's Report, Minutes of Parks Committee, 1961 February 17.

3.49   LCC Minutes of Proceedings, 1949 October 11, p536.

3.50   LCC Minutes of Proceedings, 1952 May 13, p243.

3.51   LCC Minutes of Proceedings, 1958 November 4, p686.

3.52   LCC Minutes of Proceedings, 1960 May 10, p287.

3.53   LCC Minutes of Proceedings, 1961 April 19, p282.

3.54   *Independent*, 2007 April 22.

3.55   GLC Minutes of Proceedings, 1968 October 22, p555.

3.56   London Borough of Lambeth (LBL) Council Minutes, 1971 February 24, p463.

3.57   LBL Council Minutes, 1971 March 24, p512.

3.58   *South London Press*, 1971 August 6, p8.

3.59   LBL Council Minutes, 1971 December 8, p286 and 1976 December 1, p384.

3.60   LBL Council Minutes, 1972 May 10, p562.

3.61   Five years later, there was another report, 'Use of dry facilities at Brockwell Lido': "…a GLC Music and Dancing Licence has been obtained for the largest room." LBL Council Minutes, 1977 January 26, p496.

3.62   *Times*, 1977 January 7, p12d.

3.63   *South London Press*, 1973 September 9.

3.64   *Ham & High*, 1976 July 16. See also LMA File LBB/LD/L/045/K1133 – Sidoli's parents sued the GLC for negligence.

3.65   LBL Amenity Services Committee Minutes, 1984 November 28, ref AS163/84-85.

3.66   *Herne Hill Society Newsletter*, 1984 May (no. 9), p5.

3.67   *Herne Hill Society Newsletter*, 1985 July (no. 14), p1.

3.68   *Herne Hill Society Newsletter*, 1993 Spring (no. 43), p1 article by Robert Holden, 'O Lido, Lido! Wherefore art thou Lido?' Around this period, Lambeth Council and Committee Minutes ceased being bound and indexed. Whether they have been misplaced or were never sent, Council minutes relevant to the 1990 closure of the Lido are not held by Lambeth Archives.

3.69   LBL Amenity Services Committee Minutes, reporting on the 1986 season, 1987 February 2, ref AS101/86-87. I have taken the 1982 statistics from the 1984 November 28 report cited above.

3.70   Emails from Marty Emery to Miranda Payne, 2007 February 26, May 19.

3.71   www.explodingcinema.org.

3.72   'Exploding Cinema 1992-1999, culture and democracy', by Stefan Szczelkun. PhD Thesis, RCA 2002, available at: www.stefan-szczelkun.org.uk. See also report by Sean Hagan in *The Guardian* (8-8-93) and *The Face* (Sept/October 1993).

3.73   *Herne Hill Society Newsletter*, 1993 Spring (no. 43), p1.

Chapter 4: From 1994 Re-opening to 2007

4.1   *Independent London*, 1994 May 30: Brockwell Park Lido back in the pink."

4.2   'Notes from a Meeting with Paul McGlone,' 2001 November 6, BLU Archive.

4.3   A4 flyer, BLU Archive.

4.4   'Brockwell Park Leisure Development Opportunity – Information Brief', prepared by Torkildsen Barclay. BLU Archive.

4.5   Notes from BLU, for reference at meeting of Lambeth Steering Group with Lambeth Councillors, 2003 March 5, 18.30, Room 125, Lambeth Town Hall. BLU Archive.

4.6   See Chapter 2 and Footnote.[2.34]

WHAT I LIKE ABOUT LIDO What I most associate with the Lido is the noise: whistles, children, music etc or the voice over the megaphone, especially Dangerous's dulcet Jamaican tones! Also the smells: sun block, chlorine and barbeque. – **Siobhan Thorpe (L57)**, worker in wooden hut

When you take the layers off of people and they are just in their swim suits, it is quite an equaliser. – **Caroline Tomiczek (L58)**

Everything – pool, ambience, closeness (**S68**)

Feeling part of something wonderful (**S196**)

Appendix 2: London swimming championships at the Lido, 1947–1968

A2.1	LCC Minutes of Proceedings, 1947 October 21, p622.
A2.2	LCC Minutes of Proceedings, 1948 October 19, p615.
A2.3	LCC Parks Committee Minutes, 1949 September 30, p138.
A2.4	LCC Minutes of Proceedings, 1950 November 21, p676.
A2.5	LCC Parks Committee Minutes, 1951 October 29.
A2.6	LCC Parks Committee Minutes, 1952 September 30.
A2.7	LCC Minutes of Proceedings, 1952 May 13, p243.
A2.8	LCC Parks Committee Minutes, 1953 September 30 and October 30.
A2.9	LCC Parks Committee Minutes, 1954 February 5.
A2.10	LCC Parks Committee Minutes, 1955 October 7.
A2.11	LCC Minutes of Proceedings, 1955 October 25, p531.
A2.12	LCC Parks Committee Minutes, 1956 October 3.
A2.13	LCC Parks Committee Minutes, 1957 October 3.
A2.14	LCC Parks Committee Minutes, 1958 February 4, October 20, November 7.
A2.15	LCC Parks Committee Minutes, 1959 November 18.
A2.16	LCC Parks Committee Minutes, 1959 November 20 and 30.
A2.17	LCC Parks Committee Minutes, 1960 November 10 and 18.
A2.18	LCC Parks Committee Minutes, 1961 October 16.
A2.19	LCC Parks Committee Minutes, 1962 October 22.
A2.20	LCC Minutes of Proceedings, 1963 November 19, p723.
A2.21	LCC Minutes of Proceedings, 1964 November 17, p959.
A2.22	GLC Minutes of Proceedings, 1965 May 11.
A2.23	GLC Minutes of Proceedings, 1966 March 8, p149.
A2.24	GLC Minutes of Proceedings, 1967 February 28, p164.
A2.25	GLC Minutes of Proceedings, 1967 December 19-20, p793.
A2.26	GLC Minutes of Proceedings, 1969 March 11, p185.
A2.27	GLC Minutes of Proceedings, 1970 March 10, p260.

Index

Photograph: W Chamberlain

The Lido 1938.

Photograph by James Perrin, 2006 July 19, courtesy of *South London Press*

Photo: Yvonne Levy

Photograph by James Perrin, 2006 July 19, courtesy of *South London Press*

water polo 26, 40
    Southern Counties Water Polo Championship (1954) 97
water slides 38, 43
weather 10, 43, 44, 47, 49, *53*, *54*, 76
    heatwave summers 14, 47
    Lido iced over 45-46
    London Swimming Championships, 1947-1969: 97-101
weddings 61, 94
    lesbian partnership ceremony 67
    wedding tents 91
Weniz, Carolyn 106
Whelan, Clare 70-71
Whippersnappers *36*, *62*, 63-64, 73, 88, 104-105
Whitton, Douglas 51
Wicksteed & Co, Chas, diving platform *29*, 90
Wilkinson (Lambeth Councillor 1937) 30
Williams, Julia 63
Williman, H 27
Willoughby, Daniel Patrick 33, 39
Wimpey (George Wimpey & Co) 26
Woddis, Carole, *Brockwell Lido – 70 years on* 106-107
Wolfenden Report on Sport and the Community, 1960 44
women *see* gender
Woods, Malcolm 87
World War II effects 38
    Lidos 37

Brockwell Park Lido war damage 44
www.lidos.org.uk 25

Y
yachting, model yachting on lake 7, 13, 14, 15
yoga 60, *62*, 63, 75, 88

The future. Plan of the 2007 extension. The double dotted line shows where the 1937 main facade was. To the left of this line is the 2007 new build. Courtesy of Revolution Design.

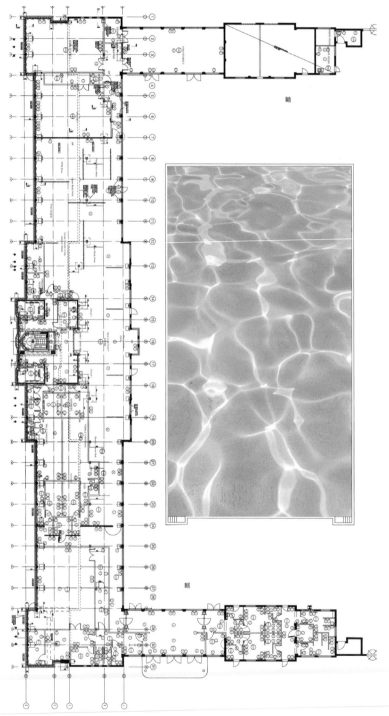

And you, what are your memories of/hopes for the Lido?